The Sword and the Plow

Religion and Revolution on Sacred Ground

by

Dr. ant

The Sword and the Plow: Religion and Revolution on Sacred Ground

Contents

Introduction

The landscape of France in the twilight of the 18th century lay poised on a precipice, trembling with the fiery whispers of revolution. The silhouette of Mount Saint Michel, that towering rock crowned with the spires of a medieval abbey, holds dominion over both the physical terrain and the collective memory of a nation daunted by seismic shifts in its societal bedrock. The sweeping gale of change, fierce as the breath of Gabriel's trumpet, echoed through the hallowed halls and cobblestone streets, resonating in the souls of the devout and the disenfranchised alike. It was a period where the scintillas of enlightenment and the daggers of upheaval danced a deadly pas de deux.

The Revolution, birthing itself amidst the cries for liberty, equality, and fraternity, did not merely shake the political edifice; it sought to unearth those roots that had long entwined the people of France. These roots, deep and ancient, carried the weight of centuries of Catholic faith, interwoven with the soil of the land itself. To understand this upheaval, one must grasp the heart that pulsed within the very bosom of France: its steadfast allegiance to the Church. For this allegiance was not just a matter of spiritual devotion but an intrinsic part of the nation's identity, a beacon amidst the storm-tossed waves of change.

Mount Saint Michel, a jewel on the emerald lace of Normandy's coastline, serves as a poignant symbol of the interplay between the sacred and the temporal. Its history, reaching back to times obscured by the mists of antiquity, offers a testament to the enduring faith of the people. The abbey's location, perched high above the shifting tides, seemed a celestial fortress, immune to the vagaries of earthly power struggles. Yet, the revolution unfurled its spectral banner, casting long shadows and turning even this steadfast sanctuary into a locus of conflict and transformation.

This book embarks upon a journey through the tumultuous corridors of the French Revolution, exploring its profound implications for the faith of a nation. We shall unfurl the pages of history, scrutinizing the socio-economic and intellectual currents that fed the revolutionary fervor. However, our gaze will remain fixed upon the spiritual landscape, investigating how secularization, de-Christianization campaigns, and the very redefinition of faith and identity were prosecuted upon the sacred grounds of France.

In the eye of this revolutionary storm stood the clergy, once venerated, now vilified, whose fortunes rose and fell with the caprice of the masses. The Church, encomium-lined in its grandeur, saw its sanctuaries desecrated, its vows mocked, and its clergy metamorphosed from shepherds of the faithful into prisoners within the fortresses of their own consecrated stones. The clergy's misconduct and profligacy had fanned the flames of public indignation, revealing fissures within the Church that were as old as the institution itself.

Yet, amidst the cacophony of rebellion, there existed an irony so keen it could wound the spirit. The forced adherence to vows within the prison walls of Mount Saint Michel painted a dramatic tableau of existential disquiet, where those who once presided over the sacraments found themselves confined and compelled to a monastic rigidity they had long eschewed. In the depths of such turmoil, the sacred sword of Saint Michael cut through the mists of doubt, a beacon of divine justice and intercession.

The ripples of the American Revolution reached the shores of France, carrying with them the embers of secular ideologies that sought to redefine notions of governance, society, and faith. Enlightened thought clashed with traditionalism, and in this crucible of ideas, the role of religious orders and the church-state relations underwent a metamorphosis. How did the Church respond to such challenges? What declarations were issued in the face of growing secularism? These inquiries lead us deeper into the heart of an ecclesiastical crisis.

The journey towards restoration, interrupted by the ceaseless conflicts and ephemeral collaborations between the Church and revolutionary forces, signifies the resilience of faith in the face of unrelenting adversity. The tale of institutional rebuilding post-revolution reveals a canvas laden with strokes of human frailty and divine providence. Faith, much like the arched ceilings of the abbey, sought to rise anew though not unscathed, bearing the marks of its trials and tribulations.

But amidst the turbulence, the laypeople of France emerged as pivotal actors in this grand drama. The grassroots religious movements, though often birthed in the shadowed recesses of societal upheaval, played an indispensable role in sustaining and reshaping the faith narrative. Their stories, laden with fervor and resilience, form the undercurrent of a broader discourse on faith and revolution, underscoring the indomitable spirit of a populace clinging to its spiritual moorings.

As we traverse the chapters that follow, we shall delve into the intricate tapestry of theological transformation and philosophical inquiry. The Revolution's implications on Catholic doctrine and religious thought speak to broader, more profound questions: How does faith evolve in the crucible of conflict? What remains when the gilded structures of the old order collapse? We shall seek to answer these questions, threading through the annals of history, unearthing the sacred and the profane, the divine and the diabolical.

The military and monastic orders, once pivotal in the annals of Christendom, found their roles recast amidst the maelstrom of revolution. Some allied with the forces of change, others resisted, and many found themselves navigating the blurred lines between duty to faith and nation. In exploring their journeys, we uncover the profound shifts and realignments that embody a period of relentless uncertainty and transformation.

Furthermore, economic factors played no small part in this grand narrative. Wealth redistribution, the seizure of Church properties, and the subsequent financial ramifications profoundly influenced the Church's role in a society wrestling with its newfound ideals. The revolution, in seeking to redress economic disparities, inadvertently catalyzed a redefinition of the Church's temporal and spiritual authority.

In delineating the political ramifications, we encounter the monumental Concordat of 1801, a redefinition of church-state relations that sought a semblance of stability amidst the chaos. This accord, a testament to the resilience of faith institutions, marked the beginning of a complex dance between secular and sacred authorities, grappling for influence in a fragmented polity.

Our narrative will not be complete without addressing the restoration of religious practice, a resurgence of devotion that witnessed the rebuilding of communities and rekindling of spiritual fervor. The renewal of faith practices, though fraught with challenges, testifies to an inherent human yearning for the divine, a yearning that outlives the pomp of revolutionary rhetoric.

Education and indoctrination, those twin pillars of societal influence, also underwent transformation. The control over religious education and the advent of government-regulated schools illustrate the broader struggle for the soul of a nation. The pen, as mighty as the sword, became a tool for reshaping minds and redirecting loyalties, laying the groundwork for

Chapter 1: The Setting of Mount Saint Michel

Lo, upon the granite bosom of the Norman coast, where sea and sky in solemn concord meet, rises the majestic Mount Saint Michel. An edifice not wrought by mortal hands but seemingly hewn from the eternal rock by divine decree. This sacred isle, at once fortress and abbey, stands as a sentinel against the tides of time, bearing witness to centuries of faith and fortitude. Amidst the ceaseless ebb and flow of history, it remains a steadfast beacon of spiritual aspiration and monastic devotion. Encircled by waves that alternately embrace and forsake, Mount Saint Michel's towering spires ascend heavenward, invoking both reverence and awe. Herein lies a sanctuary cultivated by Bernard of Clairvaux's contemplative spirit and the resolute industriousness of countless monks. In the days preceding the tumult of the French Revolution, its cloistered walls provided solace and sustenance to those who sought the divine, a refuge from worldly tumult and a bastion of Christendom's enduring legacy.

The Geographic Layout of Mount Saint Michel

Enshrouded betwixt the ethereal mists of myth and history, Mount Saint Michel's geography is a hymn to the divine, an ode to both nature's grandeur and divine intervention. This sanctuary, perched atop an island of granite, emerges from the vast expanse of teeming waters and shifting sands like an apostolic vision. Its very foundation, a marvel of geology, results from millions of years of natural sedimentation, erosion, and deposition, ultimately sculpting a site befitting the archangel's celestial command.

Geographically, Mount Saint Michel resides within the bounds of Normandy. It lies within the embrace of the Baie du Mont Saint Michel, a bay marked by its extraordinary transitions between land and sea. Twice daily, the tides—oft heralded as some of the highest in all of Europe—sweep across the bay with alacrity, transforming the mount from a secluded isle to an accessible landmark. This rhythm of the tides not only enriches the spiritual symbolism of isolation and communion but also endows the mount with a geographical semblance of spirituality in flux, a liminal space between heaven and earth.

Approaching from afar, what strikes the observer is the silhouette of Mount Saint Michel, with its dramatic spire piercing the heavens, juxtaposed against the serene, ever-fluctuating landscape. The ascent to the abbey is a pilgrimage in miniature, a physical and metaphorical climb through history and faith. Stony pathways wind through narrow streets flanked by aged stone constructions, with each step bringing the devotee closer to divine contemplation. These terrestrial passages were once trodden by medieval pilgrims who believed this arduous journey to be a form of penance and reverence.

The mount's construction mirrors the natural strata upon which it is built; layers of human endeavor and divine inspiration, each level seeking to outdo the last in spiritual aspiration and architectural grandeur. Ascending from the base, one encounters rustic fortifications that guarded the mount through centuries of turmoil, yet higher still, the abbey's Gothic spires and buttresses reach for the celestial firmament. Thus does the geography of Mount Saint Michel transform into a vertical pilgrimage, with each ascending tier reflecting an approach towards divine enlightenment.

Indeed, the lush salt meadows and marshlands that encircle the mount serve as both an ethereal moat and a fertile ground. These marshlands, known as "les herbus," teem with flora and fauna unique to this environment, their verdant expanse providing a stark, organic counterpoint to the stony grandeur of the mount. Grazing sheep are often seen dotting these pastures, adding to the rustic charm and economic vitality of the region. These salt-tolerant sheep produce the celebrated "agneau de pré-salé," a delicacy that has sustained local communities and pilgrims alike over the centuries.

The strategic positioning of Mount Saint Michel, observable from miles away, has also bestowed upon it a military significance. This geography of faith was, paradoxically, a geography of fortification. Over the ages, its natural defenses were bolstered by walls and gates, rendering it a symbol of both spiritual sanctuary and impregnable resilience. Even the most determined assailants found themselves thwarted by the tidal fluctuations and formidable bastions that formed a complex labyrinth awaiting the uninvited.

The mount is encircled by sandbanks and tidal flats that possess a dual nature: at times a perilous quicksand trap to the unwary, but more frequently a stark, reflective canvas amplifying the majesty of the mount itself. This ephemeral landscape, part sea and part land, mirrors the changing fortunes of the abbey that stands upon it. The monks who once traversed these sands to meet the needs of the mount's agricultural and spiritual life did so as if treading a path between the secular and the sacred.

The surrounding bay, itself fed by the confluence of several rivers, has sculpted the geography of Mount Saint Michel into an intricate mosaic of ecological niches. These waters, marked by an interplay of freshwater and saltwater, give rise to unique estuarine conditions that support a plethora of marine and birdlife. This biodiversity not only enhances the spiritual resonance of the mount, where scripture often extolls the harmony of creation but also underscores the need for contemporary conservation efforts to preserve this hallowed land for future generations.

Thus, the geographic layout of Mount Saint Michel serves as a living testament to the interplay between human devotion and natural majesty. Each element, whether the granite foundations, the tidal rhythms, or the verdant marshlands, contributes to an overarching narrative. This narrative is one of spiritual ascendancy, of a human reaching towards divine grace amid the vagaries of nature and time. In understanding the geography that frames this sacred site, one begins to grasp how the faith of France, from medieval piety to revolutionary upheaval, finds a tangible locus upon this ethereal mount.

Historical Significance Prior to the French Revolution

In the annals of time, Mount Saint Michel has always stood as a bastion of spiritual depth and architectural grandeur. Long before the tumult of the French Revolution shook the very foundations of the French nation, the magnetism of this hallowed mount had drawn the eyes and hearts of pilgrims, monarchs, and scholars alike. Its ethereal beauty and divine purpose married the elements of nature with the divine mystery, creating an unparalleled sanctuary dedicated to Saint Michael, the Archangel.

The story of Mount Saint Michel begins with divine intervention, for legend tells us that in the early 8th century, the Archangel Michael appeared to Saint Aubert, the bishop of Avranches, commanding him to build a church atop the rocky islet. Aubert, though hesitant, heeded the celestial command after being visited thrice by the divine messenger. Thus, a sanctuary in honor of the celestial warrior was constructed, setting the stage for Mount Saint Michel's pivotal role in the spiritual and temporal life of France.

This holy mount quickly became a center for religious devotion and monastic life. Benedictine monks established the abbey, transforming the location into a beacon of spiritual learning and scholarly activity. The abbey's walls echoed with the prayers and chants of devoted monks, each hymn and prayer fortifying the spiritual aura of this sacred place. The monastery's scribes preserved and transcribed holy texts, contributing to the spread of Christian thought across medieval Europe.

Mount Saint Michel's strategic position also played a critical role during the medieval period, particularly during the Hundred Years' War. The mount's natural defenses, coupled with the ingenuity of its defenders, rendered it nearly impregnable. The abbey's steadfast resistance against English forces became a symbol of French resilience and divine protection. The impregnable fortress-array atop the mount testified to the enduring faith and martial prowess of its custodians; a rare synthesis of the sacred and the military. This historical legacy of divine protection and earthly fortitude would become a linchpin for the mount's symbolic importance in the centuries to come.

The mount served not merely as a site of defense but also as a fulcrum of artistic and architectural achievement. The Romanesque and Gothic structures that compose the abbey stand testament to the evolving architectural innovation and the deepening of Christian art. Spires reaching towards the heavens, dramatic arcades, and the intricately designed cloisters evoke the presence of the divine, instilling in visitors and inhabitants a sense of celestial proximity.

This architectural and spiritual magnificence attracted not only devout pilgrims but also royal patrons. Kings and noblemen lavished wealth upon the abbey, seeking divine favor and the blessings of Saint Michael. These donations funded not only the abbey's expansion but also its mission of education and charity. Royal pilgrimage and patronage solidified the mount's standing as a symbol of the intertwined destinies of the French monarchy and the Church.

During the medieval period, Mount Saint Michel became an epicenter for pilgrimage. Pilgrims from all corners of Christendom undertook arduous journeys to this sacred site, seeking spiritual solace, indulgences, and miracles. Their arrival brought socio-economic benefits, turning the mount into a thriving hub of commerce and culture. Inns, shops, and marketplaces sprung up, serving the needs of weary travelers and thus embedding the mount further into the socio-cultural fabric of medieval Europe.

The mount's cultural and intellectual significance, however, extended far beyond its limestone walls and cloistered courtyards. The abbey became a cornerstone for intellectual pursuit and scholasticism. The monks engaged in theological debates, scriptural translations, and contributed to the copious manuscripts that formed the backbone of medieval European knowledge. This intellectual vibrancy positioned Mount Saint Michel as a nexus for the dissemination of Christian doctrine and humanist thought.

Yet the revered mount was also a microcosm of the tensions that simmered beneath the veneer of medieval piety. The abbey, while a fortress of faith, was not immune to the broader socio-political currents of feudal Europe. It became enmeshed in the power struggles between local lords and the Crown, between the secular and the ecclesiastical. These dynamics foreshadowed the larger cataclysmic shifts that would later embroil the entire nation.

Thus, it is evident that Mount Saint Michel was far more than an isolated spiritual retreat. It was a living testament to the intertwined destinies of faith and politics, embodying the confluence of heavenly aspirations and earthly struggles. This duality would be profoundly felt during the French Revolution, as secularism and faith collided with revolutionary fervor.

The sacred mount's pre-revolutionary epoch concluded with layers of historical, spiritual, and cultural resonance, positioning it perfectly to play a significant role during the seismic events of the French Revolution. The centuries of accumulated piety, intellectual pursuit, and socio-political maneuvering imbued the mount with a historical gravity that would both challenge and enrich the faith of France in the subsequent bloody and transformative epoch that was to follow.

Chapter 2: The French Revolution and Its Causes

In the tumultuous tide of France's history, the French Revolution stands as a cataclysmic epoch, its ramifications a beacon both of illumination and despair. Unlike mere political tempests, the Revolution was a seismic upheaval, rooted in fountains both deep and manifold. The ailing socio-economic vestiges of feudalism, the burdens of insupportable taxation, and the gnawing hunger gnashing at the bones of the common populace conspired with fervid intellectual ferment. The philosophies of the Enlightenment, woven with threads of reason and liberty, cast a resplendent, yet ominous light on the creaking edifice of the French ancien régime. It became an era where celestial faith clashed with terrestrial governance, and ecclesiastical sanctity was tested in the crucible of revolution. As the Revolution ignited, it illuminated both the sagacity and folly of men, questioning the altars of old and beckoning for the reconstruction of both sacral and secular worlds, thus dramatically altering the landscape of the Faith of France.

Socio-Economic Factors Leading to Revolution

The seeds of rebellion were sown long before the fall of the Bastille, as the socio-economic fabric of France lay tattered and fraught with inequities. The intertwining fates of the classes revealed a society on the brink of an abyss, where dire poverty and ostentatious wealth coexisted in stark contrast. To the common folk, the extravagant lifestyles of the aristocracy seemed a cruel jest, a bitter reminder of their own perpetual struggles.

In truth, the peasantry bore the brunt of this economic disparity. They toiled unremittingly, yet their rewards were meager. Their plight was exacerbated by harsh taxes levied not only by the monarchy but also by the Church. The tithes demanded by ecclesiastical authorities amounted to a significant portion of a peasant's meager earnings, creating an undercurrent of resentment towards the very institution that was supposed to offer solace and spiritual nourishment.

The bourgeoisie, burgeoning in influence, found itself stymied by the rigid class structure that accorded privileges based on birth rather than merit. Despite their wealth, they were denied the political power and social stature that were the exclusive domain of the nobility. This affluent yet disenfranchised middle class was not content to remain subservient to an archaic order that hindered their aspirations and potential.

Monarchical profligacy further inflamed the fires of discontent. The opulence of Versailles stood as an enduring testament to the indulgences of royalty, even as the state coffers dwindled and the specter of bankruptcy loomed ever larger. Louis XVI's inability—or unwillingness—to impose fiscal reforms demonstrated his detachment from his subjects' hardships. Shockingly, the royal court's expenses seemed unrelenting, and the populace could scarcely comprehend how such excesses could be maintained whilst they languished in poverty.

The dire economic conditions were compounded by a series of poor harvests in the late 1780s. Nature herself seemed to conspire against

France, as famine and food shortages wreaked havoc across the land. Bread, the staple of the common diet, became a symbol of the people's suffering. Prices skyrocketed, leading to widespread starvation and unrest. It is no wonder then, that bread riots erupted, serving as an ominous harbinger of the revolution to come.

Amidst these trials, the ideological underpinnings of revolt were birthed. The Enlightenment, with its clarion call for liberty, equality, and fraternity, resonated deeply within the hearts of those disillusioned by the status quo. Renowned philosophes such as Voltaire and Rousseau critiqued the existing order with pen and paper, sparking a new consciousness that rejected the divine right of kings and sought a governance founded on reason and justice. The salons and cafes of Paris buzzed with robust discussions on rights and democracy, planting the seeds for a new society.

Moreover, the financial meltdowns that plagued the nation could not be disentangled from its extensive involvement in costly wars. The Seven Years' War and the American War of Independence drained the coffers, leading to a staggering national debt. In the attempt to consolidate their power and expand their territories, the monarchy jeopardized the economic stability of the realm. The irony was not lost on the populace: freedom and democratic ideals were fervently supported abroad, yet suppressed at home.

This confluence of socio-economic strife and ideological fervor crafted a perfect storm. Workers in the urban centers grappled with the persistent lack of employment and fair wages, while artisans and skilled laborers saw their crafts devalued as industrialization loomed on the horizon. Even within the ranks of the Church, lower clergy members empathized with the populace, as they too lived modestly compared to their higher counterparts who enjoyed significant wealth and privilege.

As France staggered under these burdens, it became apparent that significant change was not just desirable but inevitable. The ancien régime, bedrock of medieval tradition, was no longer tenable in a world awakening to new possibilities. This galvanizing moment in history would challenge the deeply entrenched norms, reshaping the very essence of society.

The Church, traditionally a bulwark of support for the monarchy, found itself in a precarious position. Unfortunate was the confluence of faith and fiscal policy, as the Church's substantial landholdings and wealth rendered it a target for revolutionary fervor. The monasteries and abbeys, once deemed sacrosanct, were now seen as repositories of excess and repositories of corruption. The clergy's involvement in civil matters only further tarnished its image, causing it to be viewed with suspicion and contempt.

Peasants and workers alike started questioning the moral integrity of an institution that seemed more interested in maintaining power and wealth than tending to their spiritual needs. The antifraternal sentiment grew, casting a shadow over the Church's once unassailable position in society. This erosion of faith in ecclesiastical authority was a critical undercurrent in the tide of revolution.

Eventually, the socio-economic disparities and ideological upheavals catalyzed a collective awakening. The Estates-General convened in 1789, but rather than quelling discontent, it revealed the fractures in French society. The Third Estate, representing the common people, declared itself the National Assembly, marking the first step towards the dissolution of the old order.

Thus, France stood on the precipice, where societal imbalances catalyzed a transformation of epic proportions — a transformation which would resonate deeply within the halls of faith. The Revolution was not merely a political upheaval but a seismic shift that questioned centuries-old doctrines and reshaped the nation's spiritual landscape. In this crucible of change, the faithful would find their beliefs tested but also discover new avenues for religious expression and reform.

It is within this intricate tapestry of economic strife, intellectual fervor, and spiritual disquietude that the true causes of the French Revolution can be discerned. Through understanding these socio-economic factors, we glean insight into the profound transformation that would reverberate through the corridors of power and altar of faith alike.

The Role of Intellectual Movements

In the grand tapestry of the French Revolution, the significance of intellectual movements cannot be overstated. These currents of thought, both profound and perilous, provided the ideological underpinning that galvanized the masses and precipitated the tumultuous events that followed. Emerging from the Enlightenment, a myriad of philosophies and doctrines converged, each advocating for reason over tradition and challenging the ancien régime with unprecedented vigor.

Voltaire, with his trenchant wit and undying advocacy for civil liberties, launched a relentless crusade against the dogmas of the Church. His searing critiques unveiled the hypocrisies and excesses that had long festered within religious institutions. Not confined to mere pamphlets and essays, Voltaire's ideas seeped into the public consciousness, eroding the sanctity and infallibility traditionally accorded to the clergy. The Church, once an immovable bastion of authority, now found itself beleaguered by a relentless tide of skepticism.

Rousseau, in contrast, wielded a pen dipped in both idealism and revolutionary fervor. His seminal work, "The Social Contract," posited that sovereignty resided not in monarchs or divinely appointed leaders, but in the people themselves. This radical reconfiguration of power struck at the heart of both religious and political hierarchies. The notion of popular sovereignty, a celestial ideal shimmering in the minds of the oppressed, fostered a collective awakening. The faithful, now emboldened by these new doctrines, began to question not just their earthly rulers but the very foundations of their spiritual governance.

With Diderot's encyclopedic ambitions, knowledge became democratized. The Encyclopédie, a monumental compendium of human understanding, sought to encapsulate and disseminate the wisdom of the age. In its volumes, readers encountered not only the arcane and the empirical but also the subversive and the secular. By providing access to a repository of information, Diderot and his fellow contributors empowered individuals to explore the world beyond the narrow confines of ecclesiastical teachings.

The salons of Paris, those glittering hubs of intellectual exchange, became crucibles of revolution. Here, philosophers, poets, and political theorists mingled, their conversations crackling with the electricity of new ideas. Women of wit and influence, such as Madame Geoffrin and Madame de Staël, presided over these gatherings, ensuring that the doctrines discussed had both depth and breadth. It was in these salons that the theories of equality and fraternity found fertile ground, eventually sprouting into full-fledged calls for upheaval.

The shaping hand of Freemasonry must also be acknowledged. Amongst its secretive ranks, one found nobles and commoners united in pursuit of enlightenment ideals. The lodges, with their rituals and mysteries, offered a counterpoint to the dogmatic strictures of the Church. Advocating for rationality, secularism, and the betterment of mankind, the Freemasons provided an organizational framework that complemented the more public intellectual movements. Their covert influence permeated the fabric of French society, subtly steering the course of revolution.

As these intellectual forces coalesced, they stirred a cauldron of discontent that could not remain simmering below the surface for long. The ancien régime, with its rigid adherence to tradition and divine right, seemed increasingly anachronistic in the face of these burgeoning philosophies. The peasantry, the bourgeoisie, and even segments of the clergy found themselves grappling with a newfound consciousness—a realization that the world, as it was, could be reshaped.

Ironically, while these movements critiqued the Church's involvement in state matters, they also sowed seeds of their spiritual discourse. The concepts of liberty, equality, and fraternity were not antithetical to Christian teachings but often resonated with Christ's message of love and compassion. Thus, the line between sacred and secular blurred, causing introspection among the faithful about the true essence of their beliefs.

The ambivalence extended further when considering the actions of lesser-known yet equally impactful thinkers. Men like Abbé Emmanuel Joseph

Sieyès, whose pamphlet "What is the Third Estate?" captured the collective angst and aspirations of a disenfranchised majority. Through the power of the written word, Sieyès seems less a rebel and more a prophet, heralding a new era where the divine and the mundane would find a novel equilibrium.

Yet, despite the noble notions espoused by these intellectual movements, the path to their realization was strewn with moral ambiguities and sacrifices. The revolution, birthed from the loins of enlightenment, was not devoid of excesses and atrocities. The Reign of Terror, with its guillotines and tribunals, reflected the darker shades of human endeavor, where ideals were oftentimes overshadowed by the brutalities of execution.

The clergy, ensnared in this maelstrom, found themselves divided. Some, inspired by these intellectual currents, took a stand with the revolutionaries, seeking to reconcile faith with the emergent ideals of liberty. Others, steadfast in their orthodoxy, viewed the upheaval as a heretical blasphemy, a defilement of sacred tradition. This schism within the Church itself speaks volumes about the indomitable force of these intellectual movements, capable of rending even the most sacrosanct institutions asunder.

While the Revolution may have sought to unseat religion from its lofty pedestal, it did not eradicate the spiritual dimension from the hearts of the French people. Instead, it compelled the faithful to engage in a profound introspection, challenging them to distill the essence of their spirituality in the crucible of reason and revolution.

Thus, the role of intellectual movements in the French Revolution is an intricate mosaic of thought and action, of enlightenment and struggle. These movements not only illuminated the path towards liberty but also cast long shadows that continue to intrigue and provoke reflection. In seeking to dismantle the old order, they inadvertently opened new avenues for spiritual reawakening. This complex interplay of ideas and beliefs, of politics and faith, remains one of the Revolution's most compelling legacies.

In conclusion, the intellectual movements leading up to the French Revolution fashioned a symphony of ideas that rattled the very foundations of French society and the Church. From the salons to the streets, from the pages of polemics to the pulpit, these doctrines ignited a fervor that crystallized into revolutionary zeal. As the faithful of France grappled with these transformative forces, they discovered that the unchaining of the mind could paradoxically lead to a deeper, more self-aware engagement with their faith. And thus, in the interstices of upheaval and enlightenment, the soul of France found itself both challenged and renewed.

Chapter 3: The Impact of the Revolution on Religion

The French Revolution, a cataclysmic upheaval that sought to unshackle the common man from the yoke of aristocratic oppression, didst also set its steely gaze upon the pious sanctuaries of the Church. The altars of faith became battlegrounds where secular flames sought to expunge the divine light. Vigorous were the efforts to secularize the very essence of existence, where the hallowed churches transformed into cold, empty husks stripped of their sacrosanct relics. Revolutionary zealots orchestrated de-Christianization campaigns that cast the clergy into dungeons or scattered them like leaves before a tempest. Monasteries, once bastions of meditation and piety, crumbled under the weight of desecration and expropriation. Ah, such turbulent waves didst crash upon the shores of spiritual life, leaving the faithful torn betwixt allegiance to their God and the new order birthed in frenzied passion. Even in the sacred confines of Mount Saint Michel, the echoes of Hozannahs were drowned by the rebellious clamor, and religion was compelled to don the robes of martyrdom in the struggle for its very soul. Thusly, the French Revolution wielded its sword not merely against kings, but against the celestial kingdom itself, rendering the days of the faithful fraught with trials both temporal and eternal.

Secularization Efforts

In the annals of France's revolution, a tumultuous tide swept across the land, stripping the ecclesiastical vestments off its ancient roots. The revolution's fervor, akin to a tempest untamed, devoured the sacred and rendered profane that which once stood unassailable. This wave of secularization held naught respect for hallowed sanctuaries, sacred texts, nor consecrated orders, seeking to sever every tendril of religious influence upon the state.

The clergy, erstwhile custodians of souls and stewards of divine wisdom, found themselves at the mercy of a newly birthed republic. The National Assembly, a body enamored by Enlightenment ideals, sought to dismantle the bastions of faith and redistribute ecclesiastical wealth for the commonweal. In the labyrinthine chambers of this revolutionary government, a multitude of decrees sprang forth, meant to wrest power from the ecclesiastical elite and reconstitute it within the hands of secular legislators.

The Civil Constitution of the Clergy, that much-debated decree, stands as a monolith of the secularization efforts. By compelling clerics to swear oaths of loyalty to the state, it indeed cleaved the very fabric of ecclesiastical authority. Many a soul in the priesthood, tethered more to Heaven than to Earth, found themselves cast adrift, unable to reconcile their spiritual fidelity with this earthly allegiance. To the devout and learned, this act was akin to the piercing of Christ's side—a wound that could not heal with mere mortals' salves.

This dismantling of the church's influence extended far beyond the sanctuaries and stained glass of holy buildings. Lands hitherto sanctified were seized and sold, their holy purposes profaned for profane gain. Monasteries, once beacons of contemplation and bastions of charity, were shuttered, their inhabitants scattered like seeds to the wind. The very tapestry of religious life, woven over centuries, was being unraveled thread by thread, and with it, a deep-seated sense of spiritual identity.

It was not enough for the revolutionaries merely to diminish the Church's wealth and authority; they sought also to expunge the rhythms of liturgical life from the consciousness of the public. The Revolutionary Calendar, with its decimal time and renamed months, attempted to obliterate the sacred cadence that had marked the passage of time for generations. Feast days, saints' days, and Sundays were shorn from their ritual significance, replaced instead by festivals for agricultural and revolutionary virtues.

And what of the faithful laity, those souls whose lives were interwoven with the rituals and seasons of the Church? They faced a morass of confusion and torment. Some found solace in clandestine gatherings, where old rites were whispered over hidden altars, and sacraments administered with trembling hands. Others, beguiled by the promises of a new dawn, embraced the secular creed, forsaking icons and relics for the oratory of reason and the tenets of civil virtue.

In urban centers and remote hamlets alike, fervor to eradicate religious influence took root. Revolutionary tribunals and local assemblies persecuted those who held fast to their spiritual allegiances. Many priests, denounced by neighbors or betrayed by erstwhile friends, were driven to exile or martyr's death, their unwavering faith standing in stark contrast to the transient furies of political upheaval.

Yet the efforts did not cease there. Educational reforms, too, bore the hallmark of a secular zeal. Curricula were stripped of catechetical content, and moral instruction was now grounded in civic virtue and rational thought rather than divine precept. The young, those vessels of untapped potential, found themselves at the nexus of this civil indoctrination, their minds a battleground between inherited faith and the new ethos imposed upon them.

Even as the tempest raged, symbols of sanctity were defaced or destroyed. Statues of the Virgin were toppled; crosses were torn from steeples and graveyards alike. Churches, those celestial outposts upon earthly soil, were repurposed into Temples of Reason or storage for arms and provisions. The sanctuaries of souls became fortresses of the state, echoing with marshal commands rather than angelic hymns.

However, the irony lies in the resilience of the spiritual amidst such vehement trials. For every sacred space desecrated, there were hearts that held fast to faith, clandestine chapels that bore witness to unwavering devotion. Under the shroud of brutal suppression, the embers of belief continued to glow, a faint yet enduring light piercing the darkness.

The secularization efforts of the French Revolution, while ambitious and far-reaching, encountered the age-old truth: that faith, once rooted deep within the human spirit, is not so easily vanquished. Though stripped of temporal power and material wealth, the Church found itself paradoxically purified, its core strengthened by the crucible of persecution.

In conclusion, the secularization efforts during the French Revolution were neither mere policy adjustments nor solely a redistribution of ecclesiastical wealth. They marked a deliberate and dramatic endeavor to recast the soul of France, aligning it more closely with the ideals of burgeoning modernity and Enlightenment rationalism. The clashing of priests and politicians, the fervor of the faithful against the zeal of the secular, are cries and echoes from a tumultuous period that sought to redefine the relationship between the sacred and secular forevermore.

De-Christianization Campaigns

In the annals of France's tempestuous history, few chapters are as dark and amaranthine as the De-Christianization Campaigns orchestrated during the French Revolution. This tumultuous epoch witnessed a calculated assault upon the edifice of the Church, instigating a cascade of profane actions aimed at extricating religion from the very fabric of French society. In an era characterized by frenetic fervor for enlightenment and rationalism, a need arose to perceive faith as an anachronism—an antiquated vestige that tethered the populace to superstitions.

The revolutionary zeal sought to dismantle the deeply entrenched ecclesiastical structures that had long dominated French life. Behold, churches desecrated, crosses defiled, and altars repurposed. The campaign's architecture consisted of not mere opposition, but proactive, strident steps to efface the presence and influence of Christianity. Indeed, revolutionary leaders, draped in the garb of secular saints, orchestrated public ceremonies that mocked religious rites, manifesting a cruel parody to underscore their contempt.

Central to these campaigns was the adoption of the Revolutionary Calendar. A calendar devoid of saints' feast days, Sundays, or any vestiges of Christian commemoration. Each month bore names redolent of nature and agrarian cycles as opposed to martyrs and miracles. The obliteration of the Gregorian calendar symbolized a calculated endeavour to divorce time itself from its ecclesiastical roots. The new calendar, with its ten-day weeks and secular holidays, represented a temporal schism from the Church's influence.

One of the most profound acts of sacrilege was the Festival of Reason, epitomizing the de-Christianization ethos. In sublime irony, the Cathedral of Notre-Dame was transmuted into a "Temple of Reason." The once hallowed halls, graced by the solemn whispers of prayers, now echoed with the din of revelry. Statues of saints were supplanted by figures that celebrated Liberty, Reason, and Republic. The altar—a sacred space offering solace to innumerable supplications—hosted allegorical ceremonies steeped in satire.

Imposing these radical transformations required administrative edicts and public ceremonies, but also a contagion of ideas. Propaganda, in its nascent form, played an instrumental role. Pamphlets, placards, and announcements infiltrated every corner of urban and rural France, disseminating the dogma of secularism and rationality. Effigies of saints were ruthlessly supplanted by "republican goddesses," embodying this new societal paradigm.

The forced abdication of the clergy encapsulated the campaign's cruel heartbeat. Civil Constitution of the Clergy mandated an oath of loyalty to the state, a decree anathema to the conscience of many clerics. Refusal invited persecution and martyrdom. A tragic irony unfolded: spiritual shepherds transformed into prisoners, sinners within confined walls, their sacred vows crucified by mandates of a nascent republic.

This orchestrated desecration was not limited to symbolic gestures alone —terrifying and real consequences also abounded. Priests endured excruciations, driven into hiding or forced to flee across borders. Cloisters and convents, once sanctuaries of contemplation and chastity, were now defiled or dismantled. Libraries were pillaged and relics razed. The sale of ecclesiastical lands, a sacrilegious transaction, further diminished the Church's temporal power.

While these campaigns aimed to unshackle the people from ecclesiastical tyranny, they often bore witness to a sublime paradox. The more fiercely the revolutionary zeal endeavoured to expunge Christianity, the more vivid the consequent suffering evoked empathy and a poignant yearning for return to the familiar solace of faith. The bells of Notre-Dame might have been silenced, but their absence reverberated louder still in the hearts of the faithful.

It is worth contemplating the socio-political dynamics that perpetuated and sustained this de-Christianization. The Jacobin leadership, synonymous with radical revolutionary doctrine, conjectured that true liberty could only flourish in a soil devoid of religious hegemony. Denouncing the

Church as an ally of ancient regimens and tyranny, they argued vehemently for its complete eradication. The apparatus of the state wielded its newfound authority, and the machinations of de-Christianization became inexorable.

Yet, even amidst these dark proceedings, sparks of resistance glistened defiantly. In covert chapels and secret gatherings, the hushed hymns continued. Acts of subversion by the faithful—smuggling consecrated hosts, clandestine masses, and secret baptisms—attested to an undying devotion. These counter-movements, though perilous, underscored an innate resilience that foreshadowed the eventual restoration of religious practice.

In examining the human cost, we find untold stories of martyrs whose indomitable spirits depicted a poignant resistance to the campaigns. Figures like Jean-Baptiste de la Salle and Madeleine Barat stand emblazoned in history, bearing witness to their unfeigned convictions. These sacrifices, chronicled and retold, later energized a multitude to reconnect with their theological roots in the post-revolution period. As the skirmish lines blurred between persecution and passenger, the seeds of ultimate restoration were sown in these very acts of courageous defiance.

The De-Christianization Campaigns, notwithstanding their immediate effects, could not abrogate the intrinsic spirituality of the French people. The Enlightenment might have kindled a blaze, but the embers of faith smouldered still, awaiting reignition. As subsequent chapters elucidate the pathways to revival, it becomes evident that such tragic episodes carved not only scars but profound veins of resilience that would nourish future generations.

In sum, the epoch we scrutinize under the lens of de-Christianization was a crucible of sacrilege and suffering, an attempt to fracture the divine covenant binding souls to sacred life. It symbolized a grandiose, albeit, futile, effort to extirpate faith from the land where cathedrals ascended towards heavens. The Revolution, in its endeavor to delineate separation, instead etched a poignant saga of resistance, martyrdom, and the inextinguishable quest for faith.

Thus, as we turn to other marbled corridors of this historical edifice, let us carry forth the indelible impression of these campaigns. They serve not merely as chronicles of destruction but as powerful testimonials to the complexities of faith, its perennial contest with temporal powers, and its resilient resurgence against manifold adversities.

Chapter 4: Mount Saint Michel During the Revolution

Amid the tumultuous tides of the French Revolution, Mount Saint Michel, long a bastion of spiritual solace, underwent a transformation so stark it seemed the heavens might weep. This sacred edifice, perched upon the tidal island, found not peace but a new purpose—its hallowed halls repurposed into a fortress of confinement. The same stones that once reverberated with the hymns of devout monks now echoed with the lamentations of imprisoned clergy. Incarceration here was not merely a loss of physical freedom; it marked a profound spiritual desolation. Knaves and blasphemers sought to extinguish the divine light that had for centuries illuminated this sanctum. Yet, even in chains and shadows, the faith of the captive priests flickered like a lone candle against the gusts of desecration, a testament to the enduring spirit of France's sacred heritage. Thus, Mount Saint Michel stood as a poignant symbol of resilience, an eternal beacon in a world intent on eroding the bedrock of belief.

Transformation into a Prison

Mount Saint Michel, fortress of faith and emblem of divine grandeur, stood resolute above the murmuring sands of time. Yet, when the maelstrom of the French Revolution unfurled its tempestuous wings, it verdant crown of monastic peace yielded to the iron shackles of human strife. The transformation into a prison heralded an epoch wherein sacred walls once resonant with hymns became reverberant with laments.

The ancient granite, kissed by the salt breath of the sea, watched aghast as the revolution, born of fervor and fury, crested upon its shores. The year 1791 etched itself into the annals of Mount Saint Michel, a pivot from sanctity to suffering. Secular forces, emboldened by a de-christianizing zeal, commandeered this holy citadel for purposes less celestial.

Within these stony bastions, where sainted whispers once urged towards heaven, echoes of despair began to reign. The transition was not abrupt, but it bore the decisiveness of revolution. Constrained by the inexorable march of secularization, the hallowed abbey was reconstituted to serve the state's grim agenda. The ecclesiastical was subjugated to the political, and the serenades of the faithful were drowned by the clamor of authority.

Detention cells replaced sanctuaries; naves became nooks of confinement. Ancient wraths, inked in sacred scrolls, might have forewarned this calamity but found no ear to heed their caution. Parishioners and priests, enmeshed in the doctrine of divine service, now found themselves embroiled in a dread pantomime—a grim theater of bars and locks.

In the spectral dimness of Mount Saint Michel's nocturnal hours, the air, once fragrant with incense, now reeked of sorrow. Herein, stalwart clergymen, divested of their vestments, endured the ignominy of incarceration. The revered cross, symbol of their spiritual journey, stood juxtaposed against the stark simplicity of their temporal plight. Manacles adorned wrists once raised in supplication, and prayers for deliverance mingled with murmurs of despair.

Yet, though the abbey's sacrosanct halls became holding pens, the stones could not betray their divine origins. Every slab, every pillar and arch—each a vestige of transcendence—whispered tales of former glory. Even in their imprisonment, those confined within could not evade the pervasive presence of the Almighty. Nowhere else was the irony of confinement so deeply etched as within those archaic walls.

From ecclesiastical splendor to penal purgatory, Mount Saint Michel's journey evoked much contemplation. Prisoners, men of faith and frailty alike, wrestled with the theological implications of divine justice amidst terrestrial injustice. Crucifixes carved into stones and etchings of the Madonna bore silent testimony to the indomitable spirit of faith, even within captivity.

The prison's labyrinthine corridors, hewn from the bedrock of belief, became unintended symbols of spiritual endurance. From the abbey's towering spire, the statue of Saint Michael still surveyed the land, an aloof guardian persistently instilling hope against hopelessness. Heaven seemed at once infinitely distant and achingly close.

In this transformation emerged a stark allegory, reflecting the broader spiritual conflict of France during the Revolution. Here, the Revolution's hammer struck hardest, transforming a beacon of divine light into an eddy of darkness. Yet, juxtaposed against this desecration was the indomitable spirit of those who clung to their faith amidst the chaos.

The foundations laid by Benedictine hands centuries prior bore silent witness to a different kind of devotion: resilience in the face of earthly tribulation. Prisoners who had donned the robes of monks now wore the chains of captives, but their spirits resonated with a kinship to the martyrs of old.

Yet, the prison term of Mount Saint Michel wore on, and the Revolution's fervor began to wane. Through the chinks in the prison walls, beams of hope filtered, heralding the possibility of redemption. The island that had witnessed the ebb of monastic life now awaited its renaissance, buoyed by the forsaken songs of the incarcerated faithful.

In time, the mount would shed its grim appellation, reclaiming its sacrosanct identity. The confinement, once synonymous with subjugation, would transmute into a testament of divine endurance. The glorious abbey would rise again, its stones sanctified anew by the martyrdom endured. Indeed, Mount Saint Michel's transformation into a prison, though fraught with tribulations, ultimately underscored the enduring fortitude of faith in the face of revolutionary ferocity.

As the Revolution's clarion call receded, these weary walls, impregnated with centuries of faith and fortitude, would once more resonate with the invocations of the devout. The crucible of prison had tempered, not broken, the spirit of Mount Saint Michel. Man's folly, though potent, could not extinguish the divine spark that this sacred mount held aloft through the darkest of times.

The Incarceration of the Clergy

The Revolution's tempest did not spare the clergy, who found themselves ensnared in the same whirlpool of societal upheaval consuming France. Mount Saint Michel, once a sanctuary of spiritual refuge, transformed into a prison where ecclesiastics bore the brunt of the revolutionary fervor. The tides of change, both literal and metaphorical, swirled around this sacred edifice, reshaping its walls to echo the cries of those who once echoed psalms.

With the rise of irreligious fervor, the clergy, especially those who posed as dissenters or simply stood as symbols of the old regime, became targets. Imprisonment at Mount Saint Michel served as a tangible manifestation of the contempt the newly-empowered secular forces felt towards the Church. Here, bishops and priests, men who had once commanded respect and reverence, found themselves reduced to mere detainees, stripped of their ecclesiastical dignity.

The torment of these holy men was not confined to the physical barriers of their imprisonment. In the hallowed chambers that once resounded with chants of the Divine Office, there now lingered an air heavy with desolation. One can scarcely fathom the spiritual agony endured by those whose lives had been dedicated to the sacraments, only to find themselves exiled from the very sacrality they cherished. The prison's austere confines became a crucible of faith, a paradoxical testament to their unwavering devotion and the intense persecution they faced.

Indeed, the incarceration of the clergy at Mount Saint Michel was a saga wrought with dramatic tensions. Entering this living purgatory, many clergymen confronted solitude, suspicion, and sustained intimidation. What torture it must have been for these soul shepherds to gaze upon Mount Saint Michel's grandeur, now their grim gaol, bearing witness to the monument's fall from divine grace to secular stone.

One cannot overlook the intricate ironies that permeated such imprisonment. Many within the population perceived these incarcerations as fitting punishment for perceived ecclesiastical excesses and hypocrisies. Revolutionaries promulgated that the Church's separation from state affairs was an ultimate liberation, yet within these stony walls, the incarcerations symbolized a strife-torn intersection of divinity and profanity.

Despite the dishonor and debasement, the clergy remained steadfast in faith. Many turned inward, finding solace in prayer and divine contemplation. Accounts of secret Masses held within the prison, of clandestine whisperings of the Rosary, serve as luminous beacons of faith's endurance amidst unendurable darkness. These tales stand testament to their resilient spirit in a time when faith itself seemed to falter under the Revolution's weighty heel.

Yet, let us also consider the broader implications of this episode, not merely through the lens of individual suffering but in terms of its impact on the collective soul of France. The clergy's incarceration at Mount Saint Michel was not an isolated act of cruelty but part of a larger agenda to secularize and de-Christianize the nation. By immobilizing the church leaders, the revolutionaries aimed to undermine the very pillars of spiritual authority that had sustained the French populace for centuries.

The incarceration reverberated throughout the land, altering the religious landscape. Communities that once looked to their bishops and priests for guidance and spiritual solace found themselves adrift. The dramatic exile of the clergy embodied a tangible rupture between the old order and the revolutionary ethos, leaving a void in France's moral and spiritual compass.

Ironically, in seeking to extinguish the flame of faith, the revolutionaries inadvertently fanned its embers. Prison walls could neither contain nor quench the divine fire that burned ardently within the hearts of these custodians of faith. Their suffering, chronicled and remembered, became a rallying cry, inspiring both contemporaneous resistance and future reverence. The incarceration of the clergy at Mount Saint Michel became emblematic of a broader, enduring struggle between the temporal and the eternal.

The Revolution, in its fervent quest for humanistic ideals and secular governance, perhaps underestimated the indomitable spirit of faith. The clergy's resilience within Mount Saint Michel's confining walls affirmed that while human institutions and structures may falter, the spirit's sanctified resolve remains impregnable. Their legacy transcends the period's iron constraints, reverberating through history as a testament to the enduring nature of faith amid trials.

While the secular world sought to reclaim spaces from sacrosanct designs, it stumbled upon the paradox that faith's deep roots run immovable, often flourishing even amongst desolation. The clergy within Mount Saint Michel embodied this paradox. Their forced reclusion juxtaposed against the grandeur and sanctity of the mount, served as a poignant reminder to the world—of resilience, of sacrilege, and ultimately, of the undying light of belief.

The narrative woven in the grim annals of Mount Saint Michel's transformation is, thus, intricately textured with tales of valor, sacrifice, and the irrepressible force of faith. The incarceration of the clergy, rather than extinguishing the flame of spiritual fervor, became its crucible. Amidst the stone and sea of Mount Saint Michel, the indomitable spirit of faith persisted, divine melodies faint yet unfallen, weaving their way through history's turbulent tides.

Chapter 5: The Clergy's Greed and Misconduct

Herein lies the tale of avarice and moral decay that plagued the sanctified halls of the Church, tainting the very essence of its divine mission. The clergy, bound by sacred oaths to a life of piety and humility, were ensnared by worldly desires, reveling in opulence and indulgence. They adorned themselves in lavish vestments and amassed vast treasures, forsaking their vows and the sacrosanct duty to their flock. This flagrant breach of trust did not escape the vigilant eyes of the common folk, whose ire grew with each sacrilegious act committed by their supposed spiritual guardians. Thus, the ecclesiastical echelons became emblematic of hypocrisy and corruption, igniting passions that would fuel the fervent cry for revolution. As a tempest churns the sea, so did the populace's disdain churn the social order, compelling a reexamination of faith and fidelity in a tumultuous era.

Violations of Vows

Within the austere and majestic halls of the Church, a grievous shadow fell upon the clergy, casting a pall over their sacred vows. Those ordained to lives of piety and simplicity strayed perilously from their paths, indulging in avarice and excess. It is within this context that the violations of vows stand as both a moral failing and a catalyst for the subsequent discontent that brewed within the hearts of the French populace.

The solemn vows taken by clergy members—the oath of poverty, chastity, and obedience—were meant to separate them from worldly temptations. Yet, an alarming number had forsaken these tenets, amassing wealth and living in opulence that defied their sacred promises. Treasure-chests brimmed with gold, estates expanded, and personal comforts were sought greedily. What began as small infractions burgeoned into flagrant displays of wealth and decadence.

The vow of poverty, meant to render the clergy spiritual exemplars, crumbled under the weight of greed. Churches and abbeys, once beacons of charity, became strongholds of material splendor. The riches of the Church, meant to be dispensed for the common good, were hoarded by avaricious hands. Monasteries, where simplicity and humility were to reign, echoed with the clink of coins and the luxuries of a secular nobility. This betrayal did not go unnoticed by the lower echelons of society who lived in stark contrast to such extravagance.

Chastity, that delicate vow which kept the soul's desires in check and focused them heavenward, was likewise affronted. Stories and rumors of secret liaisons and scandalous affairs abounded, fanning the flames of public scandal. The sacred was rendered profane as priests and monks engaged in activities that shattered their communities' trust. This moral decay eroded the sanctity that had once been the foundation of their ecclesiastical authority.

Obedience to the Church and its doctrines became mere lip service for some, as ambitious clerics sought power through political machinations rather than devout service. The hierarchy embedded itself within the intricate web of power politics, manifesting a duality that was neither holy nor purely secular. Bishops and abbots wielded political influence with a fervor unmatched even by some of the nobility, straying far from their foremost devotion to God and community.

This collective breach of vows and moral decay, festering within the confines of the clergy, became evident to the laity. The faithful, once deferential to their spiritual leaders, began to see through the veneer. The clergy's misconduct fueled disillusionment and indignation, unraveling the sacred trust that had long bound the Church and its followers. The pulpit, once a moral compass, seemed misaligned, pointing not to heaven above but to the earthly realm of corruption.

As the dawn of the French Revolution approached, the populace's resentment intensified. The clergy, hitherto untouchable in their spiritual fortresses, found themselves the subjects of scorn and ridicule. Pamphleteers and orators seized upon these violations, infusing their rhetoric with biting condemnation. The faltering moral authority of the clergy became fodder for revolutionary fervor, weakening the Church's grip on both spiritual and temporal power.

It is said that the seeds of the Revolution were sown not only in the soil of economic disparity but also in the fertile ground of moral outrage. The clergy's abandonment of their vows served as both a symptom and a cause of the larger societal malaise. It invoked a powerful introspection among the devout and the disenfranchised alike, prompting a reevaluation of what it meant to live a righteous life in a time of widespread duplicity.

Indeed, the monks and priests who clung to their vows amidst this decay stood as poignant reminders of commitment and discipline. Their simple lives became silent rebukes to their errant brethren, embodying the virtues that had been so brazenly discarded. These few, though overshadowed by the louder cacophony of wrongdoing, remained steadfast in their divine mission, finding solace in their unbroken faith and unsullied hands.

The repercussions of these violations were far-reaching. Trust, once lost, is not easily regained. The moral failings of the clergy contributed to a chasm between the Church and the people, a divide that the Revolution would only exacerbate. The genuine reforms necessitated by these transgressions were slow in coming, hampered by the very hierarchies that benefited from the status quo.

In this tapestry of deceit and disillusionment, it is essential to recall that not all were complicit. The clergy's violations were indeed grievous, yet they do not represent the entirety of the ecclesiastical body. Many served with integrity, their righteous paths illuminating a possible return to true piety and earnest devotion. They remind us that redemption and reform, though arduous, are attainable.

The violations of vows by the clergy constituted not merely an ethical failing but a profound betrayal of divine trust. These transgressions were symptomatic of broader systemic corruption and became a fulcrum around which the fervor of revolutionary change pivoted. These acts set aflame the righteous indignation that would eventually culminate in the seismic shifts of the French Revolution.

The clergy's greed and misconduct, thus, encapsulate a pivotal chapter in the saga of the Revolution. Their moral failings served as a mirror reflecting the maladies of society, and their reformation a clarion call for the Church's renewal. Through the haze of avarice and infidelity, one sees the underpinnings of a movement that sought to reclaim faith's purity and restore the sanctity of the vows that were so heedlessly cast aside.

In understanding these breaches, historians and believers alike uncover not just a chapter of moral decay but also a story of redemption waiting to unfold. The lessons drawn from these violations of vows resonate beyond the ecclesiastical failings of the clergy, touching upon the enduring quest for integrity, justice, and spiritual renewal. It is a call that echoes through time, from the Revolution till today, urging a return to the sanctified paths from which many had dangerously veered.

Public Perception and Backlash

The stones of Mount Saint Michel, long weathered by the winds of faith, began to echo with whispers and murmurs, as the sacred vestments of the clergy became tainted by the grime of greed and perfidious conduct. What was once regarded as the pinnacle of piety turned into a spectacle of avarice, casting long shadows over the sanctity of the Church. These reverberations stirred the common folk, arousing a tempest of disdain and indignation that had been simmering beneath the surface for too long.

The populace, previously reverent towards the bearers of the divine word, started viewing their clerics with suspicion and contempt. The gross violations of holy vows—chastity, poverty, and obedience—by those entrusted with the spiritual welfare of the masses, drew a veil of blasphemy over the religious establishments. Reports of indulgence in lavish feasts, possession of wealth beyond measure, and unholy alliances with the worldly powers struck the chords of disillusionment, playing out a tragic dirge in the hearts of the laypeople.

This breach of trust became a rallying cry, amplifying the burgeoning call for revolution. The clergy's misconduct was seen not in isolation but as a microcosm of the larger corruption that aspired to sustain an oppressive ancien régime. Words of this moral decay, carried by tongues both venomous and sorrowful, spread throughout the land, causing upheaval in both rural cottages and urban precincts. Faith seemed to falter as its ordained protectors became perceived as its greatest detractors.

For years, the clergy had acted as both guide and guardian to their flocks, but the revelation of their duplicity transformed them into objects of vilification. The meticulous records of estates, hidden coffers, and unrecorded revenues further fueled the populace's ire. Parishioners, who once knelt for blessings, now stood in defiance, their faith shaken, their souls embittered. Anguish gave way to anger, and piety was replaced by protest.

The backlash was swift and multifaceted. Public outbursts became common; effigies of priests were defiled or set aflame, a cruel mockery of lives once dedicated to divine service. Scrutiny and scorn became the daily bread for those who wore the cloth, and the weight of their lavish robes felt like chains rather than garments of honor. The grandeur of their lifestyles was now seen as the spoils of stolen sanctity.

In symposia and alehouses alike, tales of clerical decadence were recounted with fervor, their salacious details adding fuel to the revolutionary fire. What was once reverence transformed into ridicule; sermons found no listeners and the confessionals remained eerily silent. The respect which priests once commanded voluntarily was now begrudgingly replaced with coercion and fear.

This pervasive discontent found its way into expressive art and literature, symbolizing the clergy's fall from grace. Satirical pamphlets, with biting wit and penetrating allegory, circulated widely, painting the once-sacred as mere charlatans cloaked in holiness. These pamphlets, much like the broadsides of a later age, were adorned with grotesque caricatures that laid bare the hypocrisy of the churchmen.

The aristocratic aura that the clergy adopted stood in stark contrast to the dire straits of their parishioners, magnifying the divide not merely in wealth but in moral virtue. This dichotomy deeply unsettled the faithful, who found it inconceivable that their spiritual leaders lived in unabashed opulence whilst preaching frugality and suffering. Such duplicity severed the sacred bond of trust, turning erstwhile bastions of faith into battlegrounds of dissent.

Public perception, once imbued with unwavering faith and respect, soured dramatically. The disenchantment was not confined to the common folk but reached into the ranks of the middle classes, intellectuals, and even some among the nobility. Brooding discontent morphed into palpable rage, transforming temples of worship into arenas of revolt. The clergy, who were expected to be the moral compass, were now viewed as the very embodiment of the corruption they preached against.

The Church's attempts to counteract this wave of animosity were futile, akin to trying to quell a storm with whispered prayers. Proclamations of piety and decrees of discipline fell on deaf ears, as the chasm between word and deed was too vast to reconcile. What followed was an era in which the once-dominant ecclesiastical power was subjected to the same merciless scrutiny it had bestowed upon heretics and dissenters in centuries past.

Beyond the oratory and pamphleteering, the physical manifestations of backlash took form in acts of violence and vandalism. Churches, monasteries, and abbeys found their sanctuaries defiled, chalices turned into drinking cups, and relics of saints reduced to mere trinkets. Sacristies were ransacked, their sacred artifacts scattered or sold in sordid markets, each item a fragment of the disillusionment that had swept through the nation.

The credibility of the clergy was so deeply eroded that even their attempts at restitution were viewed with skepticism. Efforts to return to the founding principles of humility and servitude were seen as too little, too late. The perception of the Church as a bulwark of virtue had irrevocably crumbled, and with it, the very essence of its spiritual authority.

Thus, public perception and backlash intertwined, creating a maelstrom that not only challenged the individual clergyman but also the institution of the Church itself. The revolution, fueled by these perceptions of ecclesiastical greed, became a purgative fire, cleansing yet destructive, attempting to restore the essence of true faith by extinguishing its corrupted embodiments.

The reverberations of this public backlash extended far beyond the moment, setting a precedent for the scrutiny and expectations placed upon religious institutions. The once unassailable tower of ecclesiastical power now lay exposed to the winds of change, its sanctified stone walls replaced by the fragile veneer of public trust. And thus, the tale of public perception and backlash against the clergy's greed and misconduct became a potent chapter in the grand narrative of the French Revolution, illustrating the tumultuous interplay between faith and hypocrisy, devotion and disillusionment.

Chapter 6: Irony of Confinement

The irony of confinement within the ancient walls of Mount Saint Michel during the tumultuous era of the French Revolution is a paradox that reverberates through the annals of history. Once a sacred sanctuary dedicated to the archangel Michael, the fortress metamorphosed into a grim prison for the very souls who had vowed to serve the Almighty. Monks, whose lives were once defined by the sanctity of their vows, found themselves enmeshed in an involuntary asceticism, thrust upon them by the very forces of revolutionary fervor that sought to dismantle the old religious order. Within these fortified walls, their existence turned into an austere simulacrum of their monastic lives, a poignant illustration of faith's endurance under duress. In the echoing silence of their confinement, they adhered more rigorously to their vows than ever before, their piety a hidden light within the darkness imposed by the Age of Enlightenment's radical zeal. Herein lies the deepest irony: in striving to eradicate the power of the Church, the revolutionaries inadvertently reinforced the very fortitude and fidelity they aimed to undermine, etching a chapter of poignant resilience into the fabric of France's spiritual history.

Forced Adherence to Vows

In the labyrinthine belly of Mount Saint Michel, during the cataclysm that was the French Revolution, irony placed its cruel hand heavily upon the clergy. Enveloped in the solemnity of the convent's cold stones, these men, once held aloft as paragons of piety, now found their sacred vows not merely obligations of the soul but constraints of a more corporeal nature.

The Revolution, in its fervent throes, sought to dismantle the ancien régime and all its ecclesiastical embellishments. The clergy, entrenched in vows of poverty, chastity, and obedience, were thrust into the discordant role of prisoners, confined within Mount Saint Michel, a fortress turned penitentiary. Their devotion, once voluntary and spiritually enriching, morphed into a regime of forced fidelity, laden with irony.

Consider the vow of poverty, a promise to relinquish worldly wealth, to live in humility. Ironically, within the crumbling walls of their prison, this poverty was imposed with no room for spiritual sanctity. The Revolution had seized Church lands, devoured its riches, and left its servants destitute in the truest sense. They who had willingly embraced a life devoid of material possessions were now bereft of even the faintest comforts of their austere but meaningful lives. To live in poverty as a choice is one matter; to endure it as a punitive measure quite another.

The vow of chastity fared no better under the Revolution's unyielding gaze. These holy men, having renounced earthly pleasures for divine love, found themselves isolated in a paradoxically communal solitude. The abbey, once a haven for contemplation and prayer, resounded instead with the desolate echoes of enforced continence. Bodily desires, once conquering tests of faith, now became mere facets of daily torment. The spiritual triumphs of chastity were overshadowed by its banal necessities, stripped of divine context. Solitude, once an ally, turned oppressor within the confines of a cell.

Obedience, the third solemn vow, was perhaps twisted most cruelly. These men, servants to their faith, were now subjects to a secular prison guard. Where once they bowed their heads to God, they now bent their knees in submission to Revolutionary captors. An obedience borne of faith and reverence was supplanted by one of fear and survival. The clergy, accustomed to following divine command, now found themselves at the mercy of human whims, the sacredness of their vow perverted by the iron bars that enclosed them.

Even in such bleakness, their faith, though beleaguered, refused to perish. Within those prison walls, the clergy endeavored to cling to the remnants of their sacred duties. Secret masses were whispered in the dead of night, prayers muttered beneath breath and cloaks of secrecy. The flame of their devotion flickered but was not extinguished. Irony, thus, became both a cross and a salvage; it imposed a suffering that strengthened the resolve to uphold vows in the face of their bitter distortion.

The Revolution, in its earnest quest for de-Christianization, ironically fortified the spiritual resolve of its prisoners. Adversity became a crucible in which the purity of faith, though tested, emerged more steadfast and unyielding. The very elements intended to secularize the institution only reinforced the clergy's resolve to remain faithful to their vows, in whatever fractured form still accessible to them.

Personified in Mount Saint Michel's stony embrace was the embodiment of captivity, confinement not merely in the physical sense but spiritually, metaphorically. These incarcerated men of faith were bound by the irony of their captivity, finding themselves in a prison within a prison, their vows overpowering the constraints of mortal man.

To wander the labyrinth of their inner confinement was to engage in a paradox of liberation through subjugation. The constraints imposed externally became fodder for an internal realm of spiritual resilience. This, perhaps, was the most dramatic irony of all.

Thus, every angle of their predicament held up a mirror to the era's hysterical upheavals. France, torn asunder by revolutionary zeal, sought to tear down the old orders. In the cells of the abbey, however, the forced adherence to vows underscored the paradox—that decrees of men could not wholly dismantle the divine structures to which these men of faith adhered.

Lives once dedicated to contemplation and prayer were suddenly besieged, yet they attempted to hold fast to what mattered most. Solitude among the brethren became both punishment and solace, a dark dance between despair and that faintest sliver of hope. The Holy Sacraments, whispered and hidden, symbolized a defiant faith, even when the bones of the abbey creaked and groaned with the weight of revolutionary suppression.

The forced nature of their continued vows highlighted a stark truth: while the flesh may be bound by iron and stone, the spirit often soars above the grasp of tyranny. Thus, the Revolution's efforts to secularize the heart of France faced ironic resistance in the most unlikely of places: within the very cells used to suppress it.

In a turn of fate both tragic and triumphant, the prison at Mount Saint Michel became a somber testament to a powerful paradox. Through their allegiance to vows that were both chosen and imposed, the clergy exemplified the profound irony of confinement—where freedom of spirit clashes with oppression of body, and divine adherence stands against human cruelty. Through enforced adherence to vows in the most grueling of circumstances, they transformed their prison into a symbol of enduring faith.

In the light of such suffering and resilience, it becomes clear that the French Revolution, with its sweeping secular agenda, could not fully eclipse the faith of those who had devoted their lives to God's service. Their enforced vows were not so much a suppression of their spirit, as a forced testimony of an unwavering faith, rendered in the most dramatic and spiritually significant of terms.

Life Inside the Prison Walls

Within the fortressed eyrie of Mount Saint Michel, now a prison during the throes of revolution, the echoes of past sanctities seemed but distant whispers cascading over stony parapets. The irony, indeed, drips palpable from the very mortar between the ancient stones. Once, this grand edifice cradled devotions profound, now it restrained men of God, twisted in the tendrils of fate's own contrivance. Here lay imprisoned those whose call was to freedom through faith, now shackled by their own earthly institutions—those very structures which they'd been sworn to uphold yet found themselves betrayed by the surging tides of rebellion.

In these hallowed halls, the air clung heavy with despair mingled with unforeseen sanctification. The daily rhythm within the prison walls bore witness to a curious duality. On the one hand, it was a harsh correctional regimen; on the other, a forced monastic life, stripped of its voluntary piety. Here, the priests and monks revisited vows—imposed now by circumstance rather than choice. Iron bars did little to sever their grappling with the divine. Land, a horizon bound, but the spirit, unconfined, soared amidst a clash of iron clangs and silent prayers.

Upon waking each day, the prisoners were met not with the divine hymns of past vespers, but the growling commands of their secular overseers. The rituals of confinement melded uneasily with those of religiosity. Morning light filtered through high, narrow windows, casting long, skeletal shadows across the cold stone floors. These shadows perhaps served as a metaphor for their lives—bigots cast long shadows indeed, but within those shadows, grace and penitence took uncertain form. Every man there was brought low yet found, if not peace, an unbidden reflection.

The daily duties assigned within these walls contrasted sharply with those of their earlier spiritual undertakings. No longer were they shepherds of men, but laborers and keepers of their own meager corners. Weeding gardens beneath vigilant eyes of armed guards paralleled the weeding of sin from their own hearts—penance through toil, though the latter imposed by an unyielding state rather than a benevolent Creator. Hands once consecrated to hold the Eucharist now moved in mundane cadence, upturned to skyward pleas, or clenched in silent rebellion.

Yet amongst these austere confines, kindled small acts of resistance. Some smuggled scriptures, their very breath upon the sacred text a defiance against edicts aimed at erasing the divine. In the clandestine shadows, whispered homilies traversed the barren cells undetected, seeds of faith in a season of oppression. Little crucibles of faith, which gathered strength not because of divine intervention, but sometimes in spite of His apparent absence. As with seeds planted in inhospitable ground, the roots of faith dug deep amidst the gloom, anchoring the soul against the ceaseless winds of doctrinaire fury.

This prison, darkly ironic, became a crucible where faith was both tested and renewed. Incarceration, instead of stripping away their spirituality, often cemented it. Some found solace in the companionship of fellow believers, comrades in shared indignity. Brotherhood in chains seemed, at times, a closer kinship than any they had known in their monastic lives. Bonds forged behind crumbling walls, friendships birthed in factions of despair. The very deprivation of Christian charity and freedom gave way to an introspective renaissance of faith.

Thus, the prison housed more than bodies—it carried their spirits in limbo, souls betwixt temporal and eternal damnation or salvation. Each day mirrored the abrasive passing of sand through the hourglass, edging them closer to potential martyrdom, if not physically then spiritually. In this place where iron met irony, their spiritual survival became an act of rebellion against a world determined to erase their Godly imprint. Their chains clanked not with resentment but with a shared, if sometimes quiet, hope that what was broken could yet be mended by the divine.

As bread turned staler, and water ever thinner, even the mundane provisions served a spiritual metaphor. The hunger felt in the pit of the stomach echoed the hunger for righteous deliverance. Such dire circumstances tended to unearth the divine lessons buried beneath the routine comforts of monastery life. With each crumb, with each sip, came a more profound assimilation of spiritual deprivation and a sharpened appreciation for what was lost, and still more, what could be regained through unwavering belief.

Some might say these men lived in a hell of their own creation—prideful, venal, and fallen. Yet, within the cold contours of their prison cells, they sought redemption. For when iron doors shut out the world, it was God to whom they turned, as a last resort, yes, but also as a profound testament to a faith resilient. This prison, built to confine them, paradoxically offered a peculiar freedom—the freedom to wrestle with God without the worldly distractions they had once known. Here, beneath the unyielding rock of Mount Saint Michel, they encountered both the deepest abyss and perhaps the narrow path of their salvation.

It is said that suffering brings wisdom, and within these walls, the old adage bore its truth. The physical confinement gave way to a mental and spiritual liberty, paradoxical as it may seem. Days stretched into an eternity of prayer and contemplation, and nights, often sleepless, were filled with silent communions neither heard nor seen. Their faith, cornered and bruised, grew defiant under the vigilant watch of secular eyes—livid and undying, like the lamp one places beneath the bushel.

Through the annals of time, so do we remember the souls who passed through Mount Saint Michel's grim portals—not because they were models of perfection, but precisely because they were not. Their grievous flaws, their penitential tears, and their ultimate faith amidst tribulation embody the paradox of divine justice and mercy. Their existence within those walls becomes an enduring testament to the intricate dance between divine grace and human frailty.

In conclusion, the life within those confinements reveals a portrait of indominable faith in the bleakest of human conditions. It was, and indeed remains, a stark reminder of how the spirit wrestles with iron not merely to survive but to transcend. Each stone of Mount Saint Michel bore witness to prayers unspoken, hymns unsung, and faiths unbroken. Therein lies not just irony but the profound essence of spiritual resilience amidst relentless adversity.

Chapter 7: Saint Michael's Sword and the Seven Shrines

Rising from the mists of time, the legend of Saint Michael's Sword interwoven with the sanctity of the Seven Shrines stands as a divine testament to the eternal battle betwixt celestial forces and mortal follies. In these hallowed sanctuaries, the faithful found refuge and reflection, their hearts attuned to the whispers of the Archangel's might—a sword not of steel but of spirit, rebuking the tempest of revolution and secular desolation. Each shrine, a beacon of splendid illumination, served as an earthly conduit of divine grace, bringing forth ethereal solace in France's darkest hour. Yet, amidst revolutionary flames, these shrines bore witness to both desecration and resilience, their sacred stones silenced only momentarily before the echoes of prayers arose anew, undaunted, bearing the indelible mark of faith triumphant over the temporal tumult. In the enduring shadow of Saint Michael's vigilant sword, the shrines stood as silent sentinels, embodying the profound spiritual fortitude that defined the soul of France.

Historical Background of the Shrines

Amidst the tumultuous tides of history, the illustrious shrines dedicated to Saint Michael the Archangel stand as serene beacons of faith and fortitude. These sanctified enclaves, revered across epochs, serve not merely as places of sacred worship but as testimonies to the indomitable spirit of the faithful. The shrines, interspersed across diverse locales, unfold a tapestry of tales deeply interwoven with the ecclesiastical and sociopolitical fabric of Christendom, particularly resonant in the context of France.

The inception of these shrines dates back to the early centuries of the Christian era when Saint Michael, the celestial guardian, was venerated for his role in the heavenly battles against the forces of darkness. The Archangel's indomitable might was seen as the quintessence of divine justice, leading to the establishment of numerous sanctuaries in his honor. Each shrine, a sanctified monument, echoed with the prayers of the devout, seeking the Archangel's protection and intervention in earthly matters.

One of the most renowned shrines dedicated to Saint Michael is the Mont Saint-Michel in Normandy, France. This ethereal abbey perched atop a rocky islet epitomizes the confluence of divine grace and human ingenuity. Its origins, shrouded in the mists of legend, tell of Saint Michael appearing to Saint Aubert, the Bishop of Avranches, in the early 8th century, instructing him to build a church in his honor. The Bishop, initially skeptical, was ultimately compelled by the Archangel's persistence, culminating in the creation of the ecclesiastical marvel that has captivated hearts and minds through the ages.

Throughout the medieval period, these shrines assumed critical importance, serving as pivotal centers of pilgrimage. Pilgrims from across Christendom undertook arduous journeys to these hallowed sites, their steps guided by faith and the promise of heavenly intercession. The shrines, adorned with intricate carvings and resplendent iconography, evoked a sense of the divine, transcending earthly tribulations.

As the French Revolution unfurled, the shrines, emblematic of ecclesiastical authority and spiritual refuge, faced unprecedented tumult. The revolution, with its zeal for secularization and anti-clerical fervor, sought to dismantle religious structures, both physical and metaphysical. The sanctuaries dedicated to Saint Michael, akin to other religious institutions, found themselves at the mercy of revolutionary decrees. Mont Saint-Michel, amongst others, witnessed a transformation from a revered abbey into a grim prison, a stark symbol of the era's ironies.

In the face of such desecration, the shrines' historical significance became even more pronounced. They stood as silent witnesses to the clash between faith and secular ideologies, their stones resonating with the echoes of centuries of devotion. The revolution's impact was not just a physical assault on these structures but an existential challenge to the spiritual convictions they enshrined.

The shrines' resilience during this epoch is emblematic of the enduring nature of faith amidst adversity. Despite the revolutionary attempts to erase religious icons, these sanctified sites offered a semblance of continuity and solace to the beleaguered faithful. The local communities, imbibed with a sense of sacred duty, often risked persecution to preserve these spiritual bastions.

Furthermore, the significance of these shrines extends beyond the immediate religious domain, seeping into the socio-political landscape of France. They became loci of resistance against the tide of de-Christianization that sought to redefine the cultural and moral ethos of French society. The shrines, thus, represent more than places of worship; they are symbols of identity, remnants of a spiritual heritage that refused to be extinguished.

In the post-revolutionary era, the restoration of these shrines became a metaphor for the resurgence of religious faith in France. The re-consecration of these sites, accompanied by renewed pilgrimages, marked a return to spiritual normalcy. This revival was not merely a return to the past but an assertion of the enduring bond between the French people and their religious traditions.

The architectural grandeur and historical gravitas of these shrines also drew the attention of scholars and historians. They became subjects of intense study, offering insights into the medieval spiritual life and the socio-political upheavals of the revolutionary period. The shrines, with their layers of history, continue to intrigue academicians, serving as chronicles of an enduring faith that withstood temporal trials.

In essence, the historical background of the shrines dedicated to Saint Michael is a narrative marked by sanctity, tumult, and resilience. These sacred sites, scattered like divine constellations across the landscape, encapsulate the spiritual odyssey of a people navigating through epochs of devotion and defiance. As France grappled with the seismic shifts brought about by the revolution, these shrines stood as testaments to an unwavering faith, their sacred sanctuaries echoing the timeless hymn of divine endurance.

The Spiritual Significance

To delve into the essence of Saint Michael's Sword and its seven venerable shrines is to journey through a tapestry woven with both divine power and human reverence. The spiritual significance of these shrines transcends mere geography or architecture; they symbolize the triumph of celestial forces over earthly tumult, particularly during the French Revolution, an era marked by profound upheaval and intrinsic challenges to the sanctity of faith.

The seven shrines stand as sentinels of spiritual fortification, each one echoing the might and sanctity of the Archangel Michael. These sacred sites were not randomly chosen but meticulously aligned in a straight line, known as the "Sacred Line of Saint Michael." This alignment is believed to wield a transcendental power, forming a spiritual defense against the forces of darkness, a bulwark for the faithful during times of relentless persecution and de-Christianization.

Amidst the chaotic backdrop of the French Revolution, where secular ideologies sought to eclipse religious fervor, these shrines emerged as beacons of unwavering faith. The faithful found solace in the legends surrounding Saint Michael, the warrior archangel who vanquished Satan and his legions. His sword, a symbol of divine justice and moral fortitude, provided not just protection but also a rallying point for those whose spirits were battered by the tide of secularism.

These shrines, although rooted in their physical forms—chapels, churches, and abbeys—served as spiritual fortresses. Parishioners, pilgrims, and clergy alike would journey to these hallowed grounds, seeking not just the intercession of the archangel but also spiritual fortitude. The very act of pilgrimage was, in itself, an invocation of divine mercy, a supplication for strength to withstand the tribulations wrought by revolutionary dogmas.

The spiritual significance of the seven shrines is also steeped in the allegorical tale of Michael's eternal conflict with the forces of evil. This narrative resonated deeply during the Revolution, for it mirrored the existential struggle between the Church and revolutionary forces. While the shrines stood as tangible reminders of Michael's celestial victory, they also provided the faithful with a sense of continuity—a connection to an ultimate triumph that transcends temporal suffering.

Furthermore, these shrines epitomize the intersection of divine providence and human agency. Saint Michael's sword, although a heavenly artifact, was believed to be wielded through the faith and devotion of the people. This dual agency highlights the Catholic understanding of cooperation with divine grace—an essential tenet that fortified the faithful during an era when everything sacred seemed under siege.

Moreover, the spiritual significance of these sites is illuminated through the lens of martyrdom and sanctity. Many who sought refuge or spiritual solace within the walls of these shrines were later canonized, their lives immortalized as exemplars of faith and courage. Their stories, enshrined in both ecclesiastical history and local lore, provided a living testimony that faith, though tested by fire, emerges purified and more resolute.

Another compelling aspect of the spiritual significance of these shrines is their role in the mystical and contemplative traditions of the Church. The cloisters and chapels offered a sanctuary for monastic communities dedicated to a life of prayer and penance. In these sacred spaces, the spiritual warfare symbolized by Saint Michael's sword was mirrored in the interior battles of the soul, as monks and nuns undertook rigorous ascetic disciplines to achieve spiritual purity and enlightenment.

The line of shrines also embodies the sacramental ontology of the Catholic faith, where the material and the divine are inextricably intertwined. The physical structures are not merely buildings; they are sacred spaces imbued with divine presence. Pilgrimages to these sites weren't just physical journeys, but rites of purification, acts of worship that forged a deeper communion with the divine. Each stone, each relic, each corner of these shrines held layers of sacred history, becoming a medium through which the faithful could touch the divine.

The iconography associated with these shrines—with Saint Michael depicted wielding his sword in a triumphant stance—served as a powerful visual catechism. For the faithful, it was a constant reminder of the celestial promise of protection and the ultimate victory of good over evil. This imagery was especially potent during the Revolution, when visual representations of faith became clandestine teachers of divine truths, subverting efforts to erase religious consciousness.

In conclusion, the spiritual significance of Saint Michael's Sword and its seven shrines goes beyond their historical and geographical contexts. They stand as symbols of divine intervention, unwavering faith, and the eternal struggle between good and evil—a struggle that mirrored the ecclesiastical strife of the French Revolution. These sacred sites continue to inspire and fortify the faithful, offering a testament that in the darkest of times, the light of divine grace remains unextinguished.

Chapter 8: The Role of America

In the grand theatre of history, the burgeoning spirit of American liberty played a profound role in shaping the contours of the French Revolution and its subsequent secularization. The intrepid colonists, who had cast off the yoke of British dominion, blazed a trail that enkindled the flames of republican ideals across the Atlantic. America's clarion call for freedom resonated in the hearts of French revolutionaries, who sought to emulate their brethren's audacity in their quest for "liberté, égalité, fraternité". As echoes of the Declaration of Independence reverberated through Parisian salons and assemblies, they sowed the seeds of a secular rebellion. The American experiment, with its radical separation of church and state, provided both an archetype and a catalyst, amplifying the fervor for ecclesiastical disestablishment. Thus, as France grappled with its own revolutionary tumult, the ideations birthed across the ocean indelibly imprinted upon its culture, weaving a complex tapestry that juxtaposed newfound secular zeal with the deep-rooted tenets of Catholicism.

American Revolutionary Ideals

The American Revolution, kindling a spirit of liberty, ignited torches not only upon its own shores but across the distant constellations of France. This cradle of unprecedented ideals emanated from the fevered struggle for independence from the erstwhile imperial yoke of Great Britain. Moreover, it was the dawn of a new era, an epoch-wrought with ideas effervescent and transformative. It sowed seeds of republicanism, and the aspiration for self-governance enraptured myriad souls within and beyond the American lands.

These ideals—the inalienable rights to life, liberty, and the pursuit of happiness—were thundered forth in the American Declaration of Independence. A manifesto of human dignity; an invocation of Enlightenment thoughts that found fertile soil even in the French landscape. In truth, the resolve of the American patriots imbued their counterparts across the Atlantic with a fervent desire to emulate and adapt these tenets, bespoke—or shall we say divine—of freedom and democratic governance unto their own spheres of society.

The echoes of Thomas Paine's "Common Sense," a pamphlet revolutionary not only in its title but in its very essence, reached French intellectual salons, stirring minds to contemplate the grandeur of a society wherein liberty was a birthright ordained by nature herself. The burgeoning French Enlightenment thinkers—Voltaire, Rousseau, among others—found themselves enchanted by such aspirations and conjectures. They were inspired by the audacity of American claims that governments ought to derive their just powers from the consent of the governed.

Noteworthy also is the pivotal involvement of the Marquis de Lafayette. An ardent disciple of liberty, Lafayette's pilgrimage to the American revolution signified a bridge between the two insurgencies. His valor on American soil and his return to France with tales and ideas from the New World added a palpable vigor to the French pursuit of a society built upon the scaffolds of equality and fraternity.

Thus, thus did the flames of American revolutionary zeal set a transformative blaze upon the ancient throne and the altars of France.

Yet, what of the religious domain amidst this tidal wave of new ideology? The American renditions of liberty and secular governance became models for the burgeoning French Revolution, wrestling for ascendancy against the monarchic and ecclesiastical establishments deeply entrenched in the nation's psyche. The ecclesiastic dominion, once an almost unquestioned authority, found the ground shift beneath its hallowed pulpits.
For the revolutionary ethos rendered a clarion call to eradicate ancien régime structures perceived as fetters to human freedom.

The principles encapsulated in the American Constitution, particularly the First Amendment's guarantee of religious freedom, offered an illustrative paradox. By severing the entanglements between church and state, the Americans posited a neutrality that became profoundly alluring to French revolutionaries. They envisioned a France where religious dominion would no longer dictate policy, nor impose itself unduly upon the temporal matters of the fledgling republic.

Intriguingly, the ferocity of American revolutionary ideals extolled the virtues of a more profound democratic engagement. It was not a revolution merely against a king, but against all forms of tyranny. This inspiring model invigorated the French third estate, for they too thirsted for an egalitarian society where merit, rather than birthright, provided the path to honor and influence.
The hallowed principles echoing across the Atlantic thus found their resonances in the halls of Versailles, the streets of Paris, and even within the sacred cloisters of contemplation.

However, the transplanting of revolutionary ideals from American to French soil enriched yet concurrently complicated the spiritual milieu. While the French clergy grappling with the secular tides sought refuge in the grandeur of tradition and orthodoxy, the lay populace garnered strength from aspirations of enlightenment and self-rule. The juxtaposition of divine sanctioning with the nascent call for human rights created an inferno of paradoxical allegiances and profound reflections.

The French Revolution, bolstered by American precedents, thus established an intricate dance with ecclesiastic efforts to maintain influence. Revolutionary fervor aimed to erode the church's temporal authority while celebrating the intrinsic rights of the populace to worship according to conscience, devoid of clerical dictate.
And therein lay the high drama, the allegorical conflagration of doctrines amid the rising ethos of a new societal order.

This epoch of transformation witnessed among the French clergy a dichotomy. Some inclined toward the protection of the traditional privileges and religious infallibility bespeaking old orders, while others harbored the very revolutionary fervor that carried whispers across the seas. In their eloquence and erudition, they sought to harmonize revolutionary ideals with the spiritual nourishment of an evolving France.

Indeed, one must reckon with the remarkable allegorical tales spun by these American revolutionary ideals. They provided a canvas for a reimagined France wherein the church, stripped of its temporal trappings, might focus more relentlessly on the transcendental. A grand theater of reformative motions ensued, inexorably altering the ecclesiastic countenances and the hearts of the faithful.
Thus, the American spirit of revolution, once a distant ember, spread forth, illuminating the avenues of faith and governance in a dauntless dance of liberty and profound disruptions.

Influence on French Secularization

The metamorphosis of the French soul during the Revolution, spurred by revolutionary ideals imported from across the Atlantic, furnishes a portrait of profound transformation. These imported ideals, bedizened with the luster of liberty and the allure of self-governance, took root in the fertile soil of a nation primed for upheaval. Indeed, America's own revolution, with its clarion call of "We, the people," resounded loudly in the ears of the French populace, whispering promises of self-determination and eroding age-old divine rights.

Esteeming liberty above all, the American model paved the way for what would become a seismic shift in the French spiritual and societal landscape. As one French observer noted, "The lamp of freedom illumineth our path, yet it casteth onto the shadows of our altars." This illumination, by severing the cords that twined ecclesiastical and governmental power, inspired a liberation from religious dominance. The imported notion of a separation between church and state, though painted in hues of liberation, heralded a stark estrangement of the sacred from the secular.

Over the sea, wherein distant harbors lay the seeds of America's ideals, a current stirred that would soon wash upon French shores. As revolutionary thoughts brewed, the American model became a blueprint for France's own quest for egalitarianism. It was not merely a transplantation of political structures but a permeation of the very air the French breathed, altering their spiritual and ethical compass. With an eye trained towards the illustrious Declaration of Independence, French revolutionaries found therein a doctrine both intoxicating and disruptive.

The echoes of American secularization reverberated through the hallowed halls of French religious institutions. Liberty's bell, rung so fervently in Philadelphia, tolled for the death knell of the ancien régime's interwoven structure of ecclesiastical and political power. The French, in their fervor, sought to emulate the newfound Republicanism which placed individual freedoms, rather than divine ordinances, at the pedestal of its societal structure.

Thus the revolution's de-Christianization campaigns garnered momentum, galvanizing a populace eager to unshackle themselves from the dictates of an oft-malignant clerical authority. Inspired by their American counterparts, revolutionary leaders in France pronounced decrees that eroded the influence of the Church. What once had been sacred was now scrutinized under the frosty gaze of reason and an emerging laïcité.

It was in America's steadfast resolve to separate religious from governmental dominion that the French found a kindred spirit. In this new paradigm, enlightenment took precedence over piety, and civic duty over ecclesiastical obedience. The influence of American secularism, though at times subtle and almost benign, eventually snowballed into a colossal force that reshaped France's spiritual topography. Liberty, steeped in American revolution, became the beacon that guided France through turbulent waters, often at the expense of its sacred moorings.

One cannot overlook the philosophical odes resounding from the pens of thinkers idolizing the American experience. These treatises traversed the Atlantic, ensconced within the pages of Voltaire and Rousseau, burgeoning into discourses that enthralled and enticed the French imagination. In their wake, the cathedral's hymns were supplanted by the rhetoric of reason and enlightenment, heralding a new epoch where the sacred was secularized, religion rationalized, and faith scrutinized.

The American impetus for individual rights and governance permeated French revolutionary strata, forging a nexus that empowered legislative measures aimed at diminishing ecclesiastical sway. The confiscation of church properties, the curtailing of monastic orders, and the subordination of clerical authority to the state evidenced a secular zeal born of revolutionary fervor. It was as if the French spirit, having caught wind of America's breezes of freedom, saw fit to construct an edifice of secularism upon the ruins of erstwhile religious dominance.

Indeed, the American inspiration was not limited to political dogma but imbued the very ethos of French revolutionary endeavors. The newfound veneration of personal liberties and civil rights emboldened the French to challenge ecclesiastical hegemony with an intensity reminiscent of their American counterparts. In what can be seen as a transatlantic symphony of secularization, the notes of American liberty reverberated through French assemblies, anthems, and legislative decrees, creating a harmony of secular aspirations.

The whirlwind of change that swept France during the Revolution bore American hallmarks; its tempestuous path carved out spaces for irreligion where once only faith stood. The American dream of a secular republic, when transplanted to French soil, took on a hue both familiar and fierce, crafting a legacy where the spiritual and secular attained a peculiar, often contentious, coexistence.

It must be said, the American influence on French secularization was not a mere importation of ideals but an active dialogue between two cultures on the brink of redefinition. The revolutionary ethos that suffused France emanated from its avid conversation with the American experiment, a dialogue wherein the sacred was questioned, the divine order rephrased, and the nexus of power redefined. The Enlightenment, borne of such transatlantic discourse, charted a course where secularism and spirituality danced a precarious ballet, forever altering the faith landscape of France.

Thus, in viewing the tapestry of French secularization, one cannot extricate the American thread without unraveling much of its fabric. The philosophical winds from across the Atlantic did not just fan the flames of revolution but breathed life into a secular aspiration that found fertile ground in the French consciousness. By entwining the American quest for liberty with their own revolutionary zeal, the French crafted a secular narrative that bore the indelible imprint of American inspiration.

The legacy of this amalgamation is a France forever poised between the sacred and the secular, its trajectory indelibly shaped by the American ideals that once whispered across oceans and now echo through its very soul. In the grand tale of French secularization, America's revolutionary spirit plays a pivotal chapter, a testament to the enduring power of shared ideologies, transformative aspirations, and the timeless quest for a freedom that transcends both altar and throne.

Chapter 9: Conflicts and Collaborations

In this chapter, the tale doth weave of a time when the Church and the revolutionary government were locked in an intricate danse macabre, a ballet of conflicts and collaborations. As the fervent revolutionaries sought to cleave away remnants of royal sacerdotal power, they found themselves often in contention with an institution as old as France itself. Yet, amidst the tumult, there were moments of unlikely alliances—times when pragmatism softened the edges of ideological rigidity, and the Church found a tentative partner in the state. The clergymen, once bastions of unyielding faith, navigated a stormy sea of indignation and accord, seeking to preserve their sacred rites while adapting to the merciless winds of change. Herein lies a chronicle of divine paradoxes, where sanctity clashed and occasionally conspired with revolutionary zeal in a symphony both harrowing and harmonious.

The Church vs. The Revolutionary Government

As the waves of revolution washed over France, the Church, a venerable institution, found itself standing amidst the ruins of tradition, confronting a government vowing to rebuild the nation anew. The struggle was not merely political; it was a spiritual tempest, one that pitted the sanctity of faith against the fervor of secularism. Such a conflict was inevitable, as the revolutionary leaders viewed the established Church as both a symbol and a source of the perceived oppression that had long shackled the populace.

From the start, the revolutionary government eyed the Church with suspicion and disdain. The Church held immense land and wealth, and its influence flowed into the very marrow of French society. Revolutionary thinkers, like Voltaire and Rousseau, had long critiqued the power that clergy wielded, and now, with the ancien régime dismantled, it seemed time to break those ecclesiastical chains. The National Assembly's introduction of the Civil Constitution of the Clergy in 1790 was a bold stroke, aiming to bring the Church under state control. Bishops and priests were now state employees, required to swear an oath of allegiance to the new government, severing ties with the Vatican.

A deep and bitter chasm yawned wide as many clerics balked at swearing such an oath. This schism was not merely theological; it struck at the very soul of the congregation. In rejecting the state's dominion, these clergy found themselves estranged from their parishes, which were often torn asunder. Congregants faced a heartbreaking choice between their spiritual guides and their revolutionary ideals. Thus, the seeds of civil strife were sown, leading to churches being closed, religious symbols desecrated, and the faithful driven underground.

The antagonism reached its zenith during the Reign of Terror. Instrumental in this period, Robespierre and his allies saw the Church not only as a remnant of monarchical tyranny but as an obstacle to the creation of their new social order. Across villages and towns, priests were hunted down, monasteries shuttered, and the clergy either fled into exile or faced the guillotine. The Revolutionaries converted sacred spaces into Temples of Reason, irony laden in their very foundations, as altars gave way to the idolization of human rationality.

Yet amid this hostility, glimmers of collaboration occasionally shone through. There were moments when pragmatism, driven by necessity, allowed for cooperation. Certain clergy members, hoping to preserve their congregations and continue their spiritual mission, allied with local revolutionary leaders. This uneasy truce, though fraught with mutual suspicion, reflected a shared goal of maintaining social order. However, such instances were anomalies in a landscape riven by conflict.

The revolutionary government embarked on a campaign of dechristianization that left an indelible mark on the nation's religious landscape. Massive shifts in the calendar, replacing the Gregorian with the revolutionary calendar, attempted to erase the very rhythm of Christian life. Saints' days were replaced with secular celebrations, and religious festivals were supplanted by civic ones. The revocation of Sundays, the traditional day of worship, exemplified the radical desire to refashion the very fabric of daily life.

This forced secularization found resistance not only among the clergy but also the laity, for whom faith had been a cornerstone. The rural heartlands of France, in particular, bore witness to a quieter, persistent rebellion. Here, the faith resisted the encroachments of the state, with hidden masses and clandestine sacraments becoming acts of defiance. The common folk, entwined with their land and traditions, saw in these rituals both a continuity of their heritage and a resistance to revolutionary edicts.

Such defiance did not come without consequence. Those who sheltered priests or held secret services were subject to the brutal reprisals of revolutionary tribunals. The fervor of the state, in its goal to purify the body politic of all religious influence, wrought a period of intense persecution. Yet, amidst this storm of violence, the Church clung to its role as a beacon for the oppressed and displaced, navigating the unpredictability of the revolution with a steadfastness born of centuries of endurance.

Ironically, the revolutionary government's aggression catalyzed a martyrdom that would fan the flames of religious resistance. Figures like the martyrs of Compiègne, who faced death with unyielding faith, became enduring symbols of the persecution the Church faced. Their stories, passed down and remembered, gave heart to the faithful, proving that spirit could withstand the sword of secularism.

As the revolution progressed, the revolutionary government's stance towards the Church showed signs of pragmatism intertwined with its ideological commitments. Leaders like Napoleon Bonaparte recognized the utility of the Church in maintaining order. The Concordat of 1801, though fraught with compromise, marked a détente. It was a grudging acknowledgement that spiritual and temporal powers could coexist, albeit uneasily.

The Concordat restored some church lands and allowed public worship to resume, but it also solidified the state's oversight, reflecting a transformed relationship. Bishops were to be nominated by the state, though consecrated by the Pope. The Church, once a dominant force operating independently, was now entwined with the apparatus of the state. This complex dance of power and duty redefined both institutions moving forward.

Despite the shifting sands of politics, the legacy of the Church's confrontation with the revolutionary government was a poignant testament to the enduring struggle between faith and secular power. It underscored the resiliency of religious fervor and the perpetual thirst for spiritual solace amidst the temporal upheavals. As France emerged from the revolutionary tempest, the Church and state found themselves in a new era of interaction, one indelibly marked by the trials they had endured.

Instances of Cooperation

Verily, in the tangled fabric of revolution, where conflict seemed omnipresent and relentless storms of animosity clouded the air, episodes of concord emerged, refracting through the darkened veil like the rays of dawn breaking the night. Both the Church and the Revolutionary Government, entrenched within their conflicting doctrines, found rare moments where their interests intertwined and cooperation blossomed, albeit tentatively.

In the intricate dance of political maneuverings, figures of authority from both realms occasionally shed their mantles of mutual suspicion. It was not mere happenstance that such alignments of purpose transpired. Indeed, it was a necessity driven by the very forces they struggled to command. The revolutionary fervor, which threatened to obliterate all semblances of ecclesiastical influence, also met reciprocal accommodations in the pursuit of order and governance.

A significant instance of cooperation budded in matters pertaining to the administration of charitable institutions. Though revolutionary zeal sought to secularize all aspects of societal infrastructure, there existed a pragmatic recognition of the Church's unparalleled expertise in the domain of charity and welfare. Convents and monasteries, which had been appropriated and deconsecrated by revolutionary decrees, continued to serve as refuges for the destitute and the infirm under the auspices of state supervision. Here, a peculiar harmony took root, where nuns and monks, now shorn of their spiritual vocations, persisted in their earthly ministrations.

Contracts between the state and ecclesiastical orders were not unheard of. In certain parishes, clergy who pledged allegiance to the revolutionary government could continue their pastoral duties. This allegiance came swathed in the garments of the Civil Constitution of the Clergy, which the state utilized to exert control over the Church while permitting it a modicum of operational continuity. Thus were forged uneasy alliances, driven by the mutual desire to maintain social cohesion amidst the pervasive dissolution of pre-revolutionary structures.

In the sphere of education, another ground for cooperative endeavor unfurled. Both entities recognized the gravitas of molding young minds. The revolutionary government, in its quest to promulgate its ideals, did not entirely discard ecclesiastical collaboration. Certain diocesan schools, albeit under stringent state curricula, managed to weave the teachings of ethical and moral conduct inspired by religious thought. Hence, a subtle symbiosis was achieved in the educational expanse, where revolutionary and religious convictions coexisted albeit in a delicate balance.

The cultivation of agrarian lands also witnessed instances where the sharp divides blurred into cooperative engagements. In times of dire agrarian distress, confiscated ecclesiastical farmlands were often entrusted back to the clergymen, those familiar with the arcane know-how of soil and seasons. This pragmatic act of restitution was indeed steeped in ironical need, where the revolutionaries, driven by visions of equality, reverted to the expertise of those they had dispossessed.

Negotiations concerning ecclesiastical properties powerfully exemplified cooperative necessity. Revolutionary legislations that mandated the sale of Church lands as national assets inadvertently led to collaborative arrangements. Church officials, aiming to preserve their sacred sites, frequently engaged in convolutions of legal and financial maneuvers with revolutionary bureaucrats to secure portions of these lands. While distrust simmered beneath the surface, transactional collaboration became inevitable to navigate the labyrinthine processes of property rights and compensations.

The plight of incarcerated clergy also saw glimpses of compassion-driven cooperation. Revolutionary authorities, on encountering the abject conditions within imprisoning bastions like Mount Saint Michel, allowed for modest ameliorations proposed by humane overseers, some of whom were, by a twist of fate, sympathetic to the clerics. Mismatched yet synchronizing efforts brought about marginal improvements, where afflicted clergy received sporadic supplies of books and articles of worship, bridging, if momentarily, their spiritual yearnings with their dire corporeal realities.

Additionally, we find an understated yet poignant cooperative gesture in the realm of clandestine worship. Ensuing from the de-Christianization campaigns, secret masses celebrated in humble abodes and secluded woodlands often enlisted the silent assent of revolutionary local officials, who, despite express directives, quietly turned a blind eye to these covert gatherings. The innate human inclination toward faith, unspoken yet potent, facilitated tacit agreements that transcended statutes.

In a more structured avowal of cooperation, the later phases of the Revolution witnessed the establishment of the Concordat of 1801. A historic accord wherein the First Consul, Napoleon Bonaparte, and Pope Pius VII sealed a form of reconciliation. The Concordat underscored not merely a toleration but an institutionalized collaboration that resurrected the Church as a viable entity within the Napoleonic regime. This act of formalized cooperation marked an epoch where lingering hostilities were, albeit temporarily, soothed by strategic alliance, restoring to the faith its ecclesiastical dignity under state parameters.

The narrative of collective ardor also finds expression in community-driven projects where revolutionary committees and local parishes joined forces. Efforts to rebuild war-torn townships saw the pooling of resources and labor from both secular and sacred quarters. These undertakings, devoid of grand political machinations, reflected a ground-up approach to reconstruction, where communal survival took precedence over ideological rifts.

Likewise, the exigencies of health and sanitation in epidemic-ridden areas brought about intertwined endeavors. Clergy known for their medicinal knowledge often cooperated with civil administrations to combat outbreaks. The sanctuaries of churches doubled as makeshift infirmaries, temporarily blending the ministrations of sacrament and sanctity with benevolent remedies for the ailing populace.

In reviewing these instances, we perceive a mosaic of cooperation interspersed within a broader tableau of turbulence and discord. These instances warrant a profound reflection not solely for their historical import but for the illumination they cast upon the potential synergy between faith and governance amidst revolutionary zeal.

Chapter 10: Restoration of the Church

Behold, in the aftermath of the tempest that was the French Revolution, the Church endeavored to arise, phoenix-like, from the ashes of persecution and desolation. The ardent faith of France, battered yet unbowed, sought renewal amidst the nation's turbulent passage into modernity. The ecclesiastical structure, once shattered by secular zealousness and republican fervor, required meticulous reassembling. From the hallowed halls of Paris to the rustic sanctuaries of the countryside, the task of institutional rebuilding was fraught with both divine inspiration and worldly challenges. Post-revolutionary France bore witness to a period marked by the convergence of revivalist zeal and political pragmatism as ecclesiastical leaders strove to reclaim their sacred authority and reestablish the spiritual sanctuaries that had long nurtured the soul of the nation. The restoration journey was not merely an act of rebuilding stone and mortar but an invocation of faith, a testament to resilience, and a reclaiming of divine purpose. Thus, a new chapter was inscribed in the annals of French sanctity, one of penance and promise, of reconciliation and rebirth, embodying both the sorrow of past sufferings and the steadfast hope of celestial restoration.

Post-Revolution Changes

Upon the tumultuous conclusion of the French Revolution, a period of profound reformation within the Church commenced, marked by a conscientious endeavor to restore both its temporal power and spiritual preeminence. The Revolution had left the Church's edifices shattered, its treasures despoiled, and its clergy either executed or estranged. Notwithstanding, this era was not only marked by struggle but also imbued with a profound sense of renewal, as the dawn of a new ecclesiastical order began to illuminate the ravaged spiritual landscape of France.

Amidst the ruins wrought by revolutionary fervor, the resilient spirit of the faithful endeavored to mend that which was broken. The Positive acts of faith by individuals and communities alike fostered a renaissance of religious observance. Local parishes, aided by returning clergy, sought to rekindle the devotional flames that had nearly been extinguished, signaling a collective yearning for spiritual solace and divine guidance. Restorative liturgies became the cornerstone upon which communities rebuilt their ecclesial identity.

One cannot overlook the fervent efforts of Pope Pius VII, whose papacy became synonymous with the resurrection of the Catholic Church in post-revolutionary France. His concordat with Napoleon Bonaparte in 1801, though fraught with complex negotiations, served as a pivotal accord that reinstated the Church as a crucial institution within French society. This concordat was not merely a political maneuver but a beacon of hope, a testament to the resilience and enduring significance of the Sacred in a land riven by secular upheaval.

The Papal concordat set forth a framework whereby the Church could regain its footing; yet, it was far from a return to the ancien régime. The Church's lands, once vast and unassailable, were largely forfeited, and its financial resources were significantly diminished. In exchange, the state pledged to support the clergy financially, creating a delicate balance between dependence and autonomy that would characterize the Church's new modus operandi. The reshaping of ecclesiastical administration helped to mend the fragmented structure, allowing dioceses to function once more in a semblance of order and clarity.

The clergy, many of whom had suffered greatly during the Revolution, returned to their parishes with renewed vows of service. They stood as both survivors and torchbearers of faith, their tortured past serving as a solemn reminder of their sacred commitments. Villages that had lost their pastor found solace in the return of these spiritual shepherds, who, despite their tribulations, remained steadfast in their mission to guide their flocks toward spiritual resurgence.

Restoration efforts also witnessed an architectural renaissance. Churches that had been desecrated began to rise anew from their ruins, owing to concerted efforts from parishioners and benefactors alike. The restoration of Mount Saint Michel serves as a resplendent example of this divine endeavor. Once a prison, it symbolically transformed into a bastion of hope and divine protection, its renewed fortifications interwoven with both stone and faith.

Furthermore, pilgrimage sites, once neglected or defiled, saw a marked resurgence in visitors. The faithful, eager to reclaim their sacred traditions and express their piety, journeyed to such places in droves. These pilgrimages were not mere acts of physical travel but profound spiritual odysseys, wherein the devout sought not only divine blessings but also a deeper connection to their shared heritage of faith.

The theological landscape post-revolution saw considerable shifts as well. An era of introspection ensued, where the Church grappled with the implications of modernity yet endeavored to uphold its time-honored doctrines. This period saw a revitalized scholasticism, as clergymen and lay scholars alike engaged in fervent discourses, producing treatises that sought to reconcile tradition with the inexorable march of progress. Their writings became a bulwark against the encroaching tides of secularism, fortifying the intellectual and spiritual edifice of the Church.

Religious orders that had been disbanded or severely crippled found new life. Monastic communities, rising from the ashes of revolutionary suppression, refocused their efforts not just on spiritual exercises but also on social outreach. They endeavored to provide education, healthcare, and charity, becoming beacons of hope in a society still reeling from the aftershocks of radical change. The Benedictines, Jesuits, and other orders played crucial roles in both the reestablishment of the faith and the moral rejuvenation of the French populace.

Critically, this period also engendered a reevaluation of the Church's relationship with the lay faithful. The laity began to assume a more active role within the ecclesiastical sphere, not merely as followers but as co-pilgrims in the journey toward spiritual restoration. Grassroots movements gained momentum, and local communities took the initiative to restore and repurpose sanctuaries. Lay participation in ecclesiastical activities increased, testament to a renewed vigor among the populace to take stewardship of their faith.

The penitent lay and clergy alike found resonance in the narratives of martyrs and saints who had perished during the Revolution. These holy figures became enshrined as symbols of perseverance and divine fidelity. Canonizations and beatifications of these illustrious individuals provided both inspiration and an indelible connection to a sacred past, embedding within the collective consciousness the timeless trials and triumphs of the Church.

The intersection of faith and statecraft during this period bore significant ramifications for the Church's auctoritas. While its political dominance was undeniably curtailed, the Church ingeniously harnessed this limitation, transforming its role from a monolithic power to that of a humble servant-guardian of the moral and spiritual welfare of the nation. This pivot from temporal authority to a more pastoral focus imbued the Church with renewed relevance in a modernizing society.

Restoration, thus, was not merely a reconstruction of what was lost but a metamorphosis into a new paradigm. The Church, though divested of much of its prior wealth and influence, emerged spiritually fortified. Its mission, its purpose, had been profoundly transformed, reflected in the fervor with which it sought to engage an increasingly skeptical populace. The Revolution, a crucible of suffering, paradoxically refined the

Church's resolve and expanded its spiritual mission, inscribing upon it a legacy of enduring faith amidst adversity.

As the faithful congregated once more within hallowed halls, echoes of past tribulations lingered, yet they were met with songs of triumph and renewal. Undeterred by the shadows cast by revolution, the Church illuminated a path toward redemption and spiritual recovery, its essence and mission rejuvenated by the trials it had endured. It stands as a testament to the indomitable human spirit and the divine promise, eternally whispering the words of resurrection and hope.

Institutional Rebuilding

With the tumultuous waves of the French Revolution beginning to recede, the Church faced the Herculean task of institutional rebuilding. The sweeping tides had left the ecclesial structures in ruins, rendering the landscape of faith both desolate and fraught with challenges. What had been dismantled with fervor and, at times, barbaric zeal now beckoned to be restored, albeit through a slow and arduous process fraught with political, social, and spiritual hurdles.

To understand this rebuilding, one must first grasp the sheer magnitude of the destruction wrought upon the Church's institutions during the Revolution. The Church, once an impregnable bastion of faith, had seen its monasteries dismantled, its properties confiscated, and its clergy persecuted. In lieu of sacred spaces, there now stood symbols of secular governance, halls of power stripped of divine presence, and an air tainted with skepticism and disdain.

The process of rebuilding was initiated by addressing the root of institutional decay—the clergy itself. The Revolution had not only pillaged the material wealth of the Church but had also besmirched the moral fabric of its priesthood. Accusations of greed and misconduct had soured the public's perception of the clergy. Thus, in seeking to rebuild its institutions, the Church prioritized the moral and spiritual rehabilitation of its clergy. Policies were enacted to ensure strict adherence to vows, emphasizing a renewed commitment to humility, chastity, and poverty.

A pivotal moment in this arduous journey came with the Concordat of 1801, an agreement between Pope Pius VII and Napoleon Bonaparte. This accord recognized the Roman Catholic Church as the majority religion of France, thereby granting it a semblance of legitimacy and protection under the new regime. The Concordat, though a political maneuver, played a sacrosanct role in the institutional rebuilding of the Church—it provided the foundational framework upon which new ecclesiastical structures could be erected, and old ones rehabilitated.

Yet the Concordat was but a first step; much remained to be done to restore the Church to its former glory. A primary task was the reclamation of confiscated church properties. The Revolution had seen the wholesale appropriation of ecclesiastical lands, which had been sold or repurposed with little regard for their sacred essence. The process of reclamation was not merely an act of recovery but also a symbolic reclaiming of spiritual authority. Each parcel of land regained was a testimony to the Church's undying resolve.

In tandem with reclamation efforts, the Church had to confront the issue of fostering a new generation of clergy. Most seminaries had been shuttered during the Revolution, leaving a void that, if left unaddressed, would spell the end of clerical succession. Existing clergymen, often aged or demoralized, couldn't alone rejuvenate the ecclesial vigor. Therefore, new seminaries began to sprout across the land, focusing on rigorous theological education and moral rectitude. These institutions became the crucibles wherein the future shepherds of the faith were forged.

The resuscitation of monastic orders also played a crucial role in this rebuilding. Monastic life, once considered the backbone of spiritual rigor and devotion, had been decimated. Many monasteries lay in ruins, and those that survived faced a dearth of novices. Through a collective spirit of resilience, surviving monks and nuns began to rebuild their communities, brick by sacred brick. New monasteries were established, and old ones were meticulously restored, often drawing on scant resources to resurrect divine oases amid a secular desert.

One can't overstate the significance of laity in the process of institutional rebuilding. While clerical efforts were indispensable, it was the laypeople who formed the bedrock of the revived ecclesiastical community. Grassroots movements saw towns and villages rallying together to restore their parish churches, often pooling resources, labor, and love to refurbish desecrated sanctuaries. These endeavors engendered a profound sense of communal faith, reinforcing the Church's bond with its followers.

Parallel to physical rebuilding was the equally vital task of liturgical restoration. The Revolution had seen the suppression of traditional practices, rituals, and sacraments. Many had been replaced with secular festivals or abolished outright. The Church endeavored to reintroduce and reinvigorate these spiritual practices, emphasizing their sacred significance. This included a renewed focus on the Eucharist, the sacraments of penance, and the veneration of saints—each rite a thread in the tapestry of faith being meticulously rewoven.

The influence of religious orders ignited renewed vigor in the restoration process. Orders such as the Jesuits, who had a storied history of intellectual and spiritual rigor, took on the mantle of reestablishing educational institutions. Schools and universities run by these orders became crucibles of learning that synergized secular knowledge with divine wisdom. Through education, they sought not only to rebuild but to fortify faith against future onslaughts of secularism.

Challenges, however, were multifarious and relentless. The Church faced opposition from various quarters, including remnants of Revolutionary ideologues who viewed the resurgence with suspicion and disdain. These tensions often resulted in friction between secular authorities and ecclesiastical officials, each vying to exert influence over a populace caught in a tug-of-war between temporal and spiritual allegiances. Despite such opposition, the Church's resolve remained unswerving.

Moreover, the Church had to navigate new societal dynamics forged during the Revolution. The old hierarchies and feudal structures had eroded, giving rise to a more egalitarian social fabric. The Church, traditionally an institution steeped in hierarchy, had to adapt to this new order if it were to remain relevant and integrated within the evolving society. This necessitated reforms in governance, wherein the laity were given more prominent roles, thus fostering a Church that was inclusive and resonant with the changing times.

In the end, the institutional rebuilding wasn't merely about physical structures or doctrinal purity. It was about rekindling the spiritual fervor of a nation. It sought to heal the ruptured relationship between France and the divine, to resurrect a faith that had been, though shaken, never wholly extinguished. Every church that was rebuilt, every congregation that gathered, and every sacrament that was performed symbolized a testament to the resilience of faith in the face of temporal upheavals.

The rebuilding of the Church's institutions can be seen as an allegory for faith itself—a cyclical journey of destruction and resurrection, despair and hope. In reclaiming its lost ground, the Church not only reinstated its physical presence but also reaffirmed its indomitable spirit. The tears of penance and the sweat of labor coalesced to water the seeds of a spiritual renaissance that would blossom, once more, across the fertile fields of France.

Chapter 11: Faith in Crisis

In the wake of the revolutionary tempest that swept across France, the Church found itself ensnared in a vortex of doubt and disillusionment. The ancient pillars of faith, once sturdy and unyielding, now trembled under the weight of burgeoning secular ideologies. Church attendance waned as the common people, disenchanted by the clergy's perceived excesses and misconduct, turned their gaze away from the sacred altars that had long guided their spiritual lives. The authority of the Church, once a formidable bastion of societal order, eroded with alarming swiftness, leaving a vacuum where divine certainty had once resided. This crisis of faith, profound and all-encompassing, called into question the very foundation of spiritual life in post-revolutionary France, casting a long, somber shadow over the land of faith and tradition.

Decline in Church Attendance

In the tumultuous wake of the French Revolution, the venerable pews of the Roman Catholic Church faced a somber void, hitherto inconceivable to both the devout and the learned. The echoes of hymns once resonant within the hallowed walls rendered but faint whispers, reflecting a marked decline in the throngs that had, for centuries, sought solace and salvation therein.

The Revolution, with its fervid gusts of change, ushered in an era where the sanctity of the Church itself lay besieged. The de-Christianization campaigns, insidious in their reach, eroded the very foundation upon which faith stood. Parishioners, once unwavering in their allegiance, found themselves ensnared in the maelstrom of secular ideologies. The social upheaval rendered ecclesiastical rituals superfluous in the eyes of many, who saw in the revolutionary fervor a new dawn, characterized by liberty, equality, and fraternity, devoid of clerical intercession.

Such was the fervor of the time that even Sunday masses, erstwhile inviolable, witnessed dwindling congregations. The Revolution's zealous proponents trumpeted the virtues of reason and enlightenment, sirens that lured many away from the Church's embrace. Intellectual movements, with their clarion calls for rationality, cast long shadows over the ecclesiastical traditions, leading to a perceptible shift in public sentiment.

The clergy, beset by accusations of venality and moral bankruptcy, found their influence waning. The sacred vows, once held in high esteem, seemed tainted under the revolutionary lens. The faithful, disillusioned by reports of misconduct, recoiled from their spiritual shepherds, opting instead for a path illuminated by the Age of Reason. Hence, the Church's moral authority, once deemed unassailable, encountered unprecedented erosion.

Moreover, the repressive secular policies enacted by the Revolutionary government exacerbated this drift. The civil constitution of the clergy, which sought to subordinate ecclesiastical hierarchy to civil authority, instigated a schism that further alienated the devout. Priests who swore allegiance to the state were viewed with suspicion, while those who remained loyal to Rome faced persecution.

In communities that had once thrived under the auspices of the Church, attendance waned dramatically. Sacraments, pivotal to the Catholic experience, became scarce rites for many. Baptisms, marriages, and even the final rites of the departed saw diminished observance as the Revolution's socio-political doctrines seeped into the very fabric of daily life.

Yet, it must be acknowledged, not all who distanced themselves from the Church did so willingly. The ubiquitous threat of retribution for public displays of religiosity coerced many to forsake the pews. The specter of imprisonment or worse for clinging to old traditions loomed large, compelling a compliance born out of fear rather than conviction.

Among the populace, particularly the peasantry, there existed pockets of quiet resistance. These steadfast souls, resolute in their devotion, continued to practice their faith in secrecy, holding clandestine gatherings and communions. Their perseverance, however, did little to stem the general decline, which had begun to embed itself within the collective psyche of a revolution-ravaged nation.

The urban centers, burgeoning hotbeds of revolutionary zeal, exhibited the starkest decline in church attendance. Citizens, enamored with the newfound ideals of republicanism, readily eschewed traditional ecclesiastical engagements. The Church, in these locales, found it increasingly arduous to compete with the allure of political discourse and public assemblies, which had supplanted the sanctified gatherings of yore.

In contrast, rural areas, though not untouched by the revolutionary fervor, maintained a semblance of their erstwhile religious routines. However, even in these bastions of traditionalism, the seeds of skepticism had been sown. The clergy, now fragmented and demoralized, struggled to rekindle the fervent faith that had once characterized their congregations.

Ironies abounded; the Revolution, with its professed aim of liberating the masses, had in many ways chained them to an existential quandary. Freed from the Church's dogmatic strictures, yet bereft of the spiritual solace it had long provided, many found themselves adrift in a sea of uncertainty.

As the Revolution's tempest subsided and the land began its slow march towards reconciliation, the Church sought to regain its lost foothold. Efforts to restore the diminished sanctuaries and revive spiritual engagement became paramount. Yet, the scars of the revolutionary era were not easily healed. Church attendance, while showing signs of recovery, never quite returned to its pre-revolutionary fervor. The faith of France had been irrevocably altered; its followers caught between the vestiges of devout tradition and the inexorable push towards modernity.

Thus, the decline in church attendance during and after the French Revolution stands as a poignant testament to the profound shifts that reshaped French society. In that era of tumultuous transformation, the Church, a once indomitable beacon of spiritual succor, found itself navigating uncharted waters, its legacy forever intertwined with the Revolution's secular tide.

Loss of Religious Authority

The tempest of the French Revolution did more than just unsettle the political and social order of France; it struck a deadly blow to the foundation upon which the nation's faith was built. The crumbling of religious authority during this turbulent epoch was not a sudden cataclysm but rather a protracted erosion, a gradual gnawing away at the pillars that once upheld the sanctity of the Church. The clergy, those supposed to be the shepherds of souls, found themselves beleaguered, and their grasp on the hearts and minds of the faithful weakened steadily under the incessant storms of revolutionary fervor.

In the years leading to the Revolution, the Church held a preeminent position in the French social hierarchy, buttressed by centuries of tradition and unassailable belief. However, this once-unquestionable authority began to falter under the weight of Enlightenment ideals and burgeoning secularism. The thinkers and philosophers of the age championed reason over revelation, fostering a skeptical public increasingly disenchanted with clerical power. The Church's moral and spiritual supremacy was no longer seen as sacrosanct but as an institution in need of reform and, for some, abolition.

With the ousting of the monarchy came a militant de-Christianization movement that sought to sever the Church from the state and strip it of its temporal power. The Civil Constitution of the Clergy (1790) mandated that clergymen swear an oath of loyalty to the revolution, placing them in direct opposition to their spiritual allegiance to Rome. This divisive edict created a schism within the clergy, between those who complied and became known as "jurors" and those who resisted, labeled as "refractory" priests. This internecine conflict further splintered the Church, scattering its influence asunder like leaves before a relentless gale.

Under the escalated fervor of revolution, churches were despoiled, icons destroyed, and sacraments neglected. The landscape of faith was transformed into a barren terrain, with altars overturned and chalices emptied of their sanctity. Even Mount Saint Michel, once a bastion of monastic devotion, was not spared from the desecration, its holy precincts repurposed brutally as cells for incarcerating clergy. This repurposing signified more than just a physical transformation; it symbolized the profound and abiding condemnation of the ecclesiastical authority that had once dominated the spiritual and temporal realms.

Amidst the disarray and systematic dismantling of religious structures, the resonance of the Church's moral voice waned. Parishioners disillusioned by the Church's alignment with the ancien régime now found solace in secular ideologies, while others drifted in a spiritual limbo. The attendance at Mass dwindled, pews that once brimmed with the devout now lay empty, the echoes of prayers and hymns replaced by an unsettling silence that hung like a pall over the cathedrals and chapels.

The Church's loss of authority was also compounded by the misconduct and perceived avarice of its clerics. Reports of violations of vows and the opulence enjoyed by high-ranking officials only served to tarnish the Church's image further. These tales of moral decay and betrayal fed the revolutionary zeal, providing ammunition for those who sought to sever the link between France's destiny and the Church's dominion. The once-revered shepherds were now seen as wolves in sheep's clothing, their spiritual authority eroded to naught.

As the Church's grip loosened, a new civil religion emerged, one that exalted the principles of liberty, equality, and fraternity. The festival of the Supreme Being, orchestrated by Robespierre, exemplified this new secular spirituality that sought to replace Christianity with the veneration of reason and republican virtue. Statues of saints were supplanted by busts of revolutionary heroes; prayers once directed to divine providence were now composed for the nation-state. The ecclesiastical hierarchy found itself displaced in the public consciousness by a nascent civic theology.

However, the erosion of religious authority did not extinguish the flame of faith within the hearts of all. In the hinterlands and hidden quarters, pockets of clandestine worship persisted, shepherded by refractory priests who defied the revolutionary decrees. These acts of quiet resistance kept the embers of Catholic devotion alive, even amidst the hostile winds of de-Christianization. The underground Masses and secret sacraments became beacons of hope for the faithful, a testament to the enduring resilience of the spiritual over the temporal.

The Revolution's relentless assault on the Church brought to the fore an irony of profound magnitude. In attempting to eradicate the Church's influence, the revolutionaries inadvertently underscored the very importance of spiritual life to the social fabric of France. The ensuing faith crisis highlighted a deeper existential void that mere secular dogma could not fill. Despite the fervent attempts to deconstruct traditional religiosity, the human spirit's intrinsic yearning for the divine remained inexorable.

Although the Napoleonic Concordat of 1801 sought to mend the fractures between the Church and the state, the restoration was but a shadow of the former ecclesiastical authority. The Church emerged from the Revolution diminished and redefined, its influence curtailed by the new sociopolitical landscape. It struggled to reclaim its role as the arbiter of moral and spiritual life in France, navigating a post-revolutionary world where religious faith had been profoundly shaken.

In conclusion, the French Revolution was a crucible that tested the Church's authority to breaking point. What emerged from this ordeal was a profoundly altered ecclesiastical landscape, one where the sacred authority of old was irrevocably transformed. The Revolution, in severing the ties between the Church and state, exposed the fragile foundation upon which religious authority had rested, unveiling the intricate dance of power, faith, and identity that would continue to shape France's spiritual path in the years to come.

Chapter 12: Symbolism of Mount Saint Michel

Amidst the swirling mists of history, Mount Saint Michel emerges as a divine beacon, straddling the realms of sacred and secular with an enigmatic allure. This venerable mount, crowned with a celestial abbey, speaks volumes about the indomitable spirit of France. During the tumult of the French Revolution, it stood as an immutable symbol of piety engulfed by the winds of change, encapsulating the nation's struggle between faith and enlightenment. As the tides of secularism ebbed and flowed, Mount Saint Michel's resilient spire pierced the heavens, a silent testament to the enduring essence of a beleaguered yet steadfast national character. It is in this crucible of conflict and sanctity that the mount's true significance reveals itself: an emblem of France's dual soul, ever oscillating between the divine grace bestowed by Saint Michael and the fervent pursuit of liberty and progress. This juxtaposition, teetering poetically on the edge of the natural and supernatural, reveals the heart of a country striving to reconcile its illustrious, devout past with the spirit of revolutionary change.

The Sacred and the Secular

In the shadowed grandeur of Mount Saint Michel, there thrives a compelling interplay between the sacred and the secular. Perched upon rugged rock, the monastery stands as a sentinel of spiritual aspiration, watched over by the Archangel Michael, whose sword gleams with divine justice. However, this same edifice has witnessed, endured, and been transformed by secular forces, especially during the seismic upheavals of the French Revolution. A study of this transformation reveals not just the tangible shifts in stone and sanctity, but also the ephemeral dance between faith and statecraft.

The Benedictine monks first claimed these shores, imbuing the mount with a sanctity that resonated outward into the heart of Christendom. Their chants, lifted skyward through hallowed cloisters, sought to pierce the heavens, a testament to human piety. But as centuries passed, the Revolution converged upon Mount Saint Michel, bringing with it the fervor of secularism. The serene sanctity of the monastery was disrupted, its sacred chambers echoed with the clamor of defiance against ecclesiastical authority.

The sacredness of the mount can be traced to its very inception. Tradition holds that in the early 8th century, Saint Michael appeared to Saint Aubert, bishop of Avranches, instructing him to build an oratory in his honor atop the mount. The vision, striking and divine, was more than a mere apparition; it was a celestial command, which imbued the very stones with a sanctified purpose. This divine mandate stood in stark contrast to the secular tide that would later claim the mount.

Unlike other sacred sites, whose sanctity was solely derived from human veneration, Mount Saint Michel held a compounded sacredness due to its celestial endorsement. As monks and pilgrims journeyed to its heights, they were not merely ascending a hill; they were scaling a stairway to heaven, a conduit between the earthly realm and the divine.

Yet, as the revolution swirled through France, a profound secularization campaign sought to erode the bedrock of faith. Mount Saint Michel bore witness to these tides of secularism, wherein the clergymen, once venerable stewards of sacred rites, found themselves at odds with revolutionary fervor. The symbol of divine guardianship became a mundane tool in the machinations of state power. Monastic tranquility was shattered, and the walls that once confined piety now imprisoned discontent.

The sacred and the secular clashed in an allegorical battle, with Mount Saint Michel as the battleground. The sacred halls, echoing with prayers for centuries, were repurposed for secular uses, serving as a prison. The transformation of this spiritual refuge into a penitentiary served as a stark symbol of the revolution's intent to usurp religious authority and emphasize the dominion of rational, secular governance.

This shift did not merely signify a change in physical structure but reflected a profound philosophical metamorphosis. The mount, originally a beacon of divine splendor, witnessed the encroachment of secular ideologies that sought to redefine the role of spirituality in public life. Incarcerating clergy within these sacred grounds was both a literal and figurative statement against the established religious order.

When the sacred architecture of Mount Saint Michel was repurposed for secular imprisonment, it symbolized the relegation of the divine to the mundane. The divine sanctity of the abbey, ringed by angelic visions, now hosted earthly trials and tribulations. The monks' solemn vows, once shielded beneath the aegis of celestial grace, stood exposed to the scrutinizing lens of secular law. The ethereal aura, which had cloaked the mount in divine light, dimmed under the shadow of pragmatic revolution. This dualism marked a poignant chapter in the long saga of Mount Saint Michel.

The transformation underscored the broader secular agenda that sought to diminish the church's influence, equating divine sanctity with human fallibility. Through the lens of Mount Saint Michel, one perceives how the sacred was systematically desacralized, reduced to mere historical relics, and refashioned for utilitarian purposes. This pragmatic reconfiguration was emblematic of the broader secular shifts reshaping France.

The duality of Mount Saint Michel during this period also served as a poignant symbol of the overarching struggle between entrenched spiritual authority and burgeoning secular power. The once-unquestionable sanctity of the mount faced direct opposition from the relentless advance of secular rationality. The monastery's transformation into a prison for the clergy became an emblem of this seismic shift.

Yet, the sacred could not be entirely extinguished. Within these very walls where once resided the divine, sparks of spiritual resilience flickered. The imprisoned clergy, stripped of their sanctified roles, continued their devotion clandestinely. Their clandestine worship within the secularized confines of their imprisonment underscored the enduring potency of faith amid the iron grasp of secularism. This clandestine devotion, albeit shrouded in secrecy, resonated with an ineffable essence, reminding all of the indomitable spirit of faith.

As the tides of revolution ebbed, the mount slowly reclaimed its sacred essence. Its harsh tenure as a penitentiary subsided, giving way to a rekindling of its spiritual purpose. The divine call once heeded by Saint Aubert reverberated anew, a testament to the undying sacredness that time and trial could not erase. The mount's duality—sacred and secular—stood as a beacon of the eternal struggle for the soul of a nation.

The syzygy of sacred and secular at Mount Saint Michel serves as a microcosm of the broader contest between the church and the revolutionary state. Here, the celestial and terrestrial converged, bringing forth a mosaic of contrasts and coexistence. The divine and the mundane, locked in an unending dance, where each step reflects centuries of conflict, collaboration, and coalescence.

In conclusion, Mount Saint Michel's compelling duality as both a divine sanctuary and a tool of secular power encapsulates the tumultuous narrative of the French Revolution. The sacred and the secular trajectories converged, clashed, and coalesced within its hallowed halls. The mount stands as a testament to the enduring struggle and eventual reconciliation between the divine virtues of faith and the inexorable march of secular rationality. This confluence of sanctity and secularism offers a profound perspective on the broader implications of the French Revolution, reflecting the perennial tension between spiritual aspiration and worldly governance.

Representing National Character

Mount Saint Michel, a beacon of enduring faith and unrelenting spirit, stands as a testament to the essence of French identity. This awe-inspiring edifice, arising majestically from the waves, embodies not merely the religious fervor of the nation, but the very soul of its people. As both refuge and fortress, it has sheltered the faithful through turbulent epochs, its stone walls echoing the prayers and pleas of countless generations.

Indeed, the representation of national character within the confines of Mount Saint Michel is vividly illustrated through its dual role as a sacred sanctuary and a symbol of resilience. During the Revolution, as secular forces sought to dismantle the sanctity of religious institutions, the fortitude of the Abbey's structure, and its continued spiritual significance, mirrored the indomitable will of the French populace. Through these acts of perseverance, Mount Saint Michel became more than a geographical landmark; it evolved into a potent emblem of resistance against oppression.

In the very stones of the island rises an allegorical image of France itself —a nation striving between reverence and revolution. The transformation of Mount Saint Michel into a prison during the Revolution can be seen as a microcosm of the broader national conflict. While the monastery's cloisters were converted into cells, the spirit of Saint Michael, the angelic protector, continued to inspire those within and without its ancient walls. This dichotomy, of holiness perverted yet never wholly eradicated, speaks volumes about the character of a France caught between the old and the new, sanctity and secularism.

The inherent tension between the sacred and the secular on Mount Saint Michel is a reflection of the broader societal turbulence. The French Revolution, with its radical de-Christianization campaigns, attempted to strip the nation of its religious garments. Yet, the mountain itself, steadfast and immutable, stood as a bulwark against the tides of change. The burning fervor of faith, simmering beneath the surface of political upheaval, is emblematic of the French spirit that cannot readily sever its spiritual roots, despite the forces that press upon it.

The anecdotal reveries of Mount Saint Michel do more than recount history—they reflect the inner conflict of a nation torn between its devout past and tumultuous present. The site's endurance serves as an allegory for the resilient nature of French devotion. At the heart of this lies a powerful narrative: though the Revolution sought to imprison the clergy and silence the chant of prayers, the celestial resonance of Saint Michael's sword pierced the veils of oppression, embodying the triumph of the divine spirit over temporal adversity.

While many French people welcomed the swift winds of change brought by the Revolution, there remained a deep-seated reverence for the sacred, an intrinsic part of their very being. Mount Saint Michel, thus, becomes a powerful narrative device, illustrating the layered and often contradictory nature of French identity. In its steadfastness, one finds an unspoken acknowledgment of the sacred that resides in the heart of every French soul, an aspect of national character that no revolution can wholly expunge.

Moreover, the veneration of Saint Michael himself serves to highlight the virtues esteemed in the national psyche—valor, sanctity, and justice. The archangel, often depicted vanquishing evil, speaks to a collective ideal of righteousness and moral fortitude that the French people have long aspired to. In Mount Saint Michel's silent, watchful presence, there is a continuous call to virtuous action, a beckoning towards a higher moral plane, reflecting a deep-seated belief in the triumph of good over evil.

Mount Saint Michel's story during the Revolution is not merely one of architectural resilience but of existential struggle. It stands as a symbol of the convoluted journey of a nation, embodying the duality of seeking enlightenment while cherishing tradition. The tales encased within its weathered stone serve as a poignant reminder of the national character, wherein the past and the future coalesce in a delicate dance between reverence and rebellion.

In conclusion, Mount Saint Michel, during and after the Revolution, encapsulates the quintessence of French national character. It is a place where faith and freedom converge, where the past is not mere memory but an active, living presence that informs and molds the character of the present. Its enduring significance illuminates the steadfast spirit of the French people, who, amidst the fiercest storms of change, hold fast to a sacred identity that is as immutable as the rock on which Mount Saint Michel stands.

Chapter 13: The Hierarchy's Response

As the tempest of revolution sought to sweep away the ecclesiastical foundations, the Church's hierarchy arose with fervor and gravity to reclaim its sacred dominion. Heads of the Church, once shielded by sanctity and tradition, now stood vulnerable yet resolute. They wielded the pen with sanctified intent, issuing decrees that roared with divine authority amid a landscape marred by secular upheaval. Eminences and prelates undertook the solemn task of reasserting their influence, invoking the sanctity of ancient rites as bulwarks against a world teetering towards godlessness. Through pastoral letters and synodal declarations, the divine lineage of episcopal command endeavored to rekindle the embers of faith within France's beleaguered souls. The hierarchy's stalwart proclamations echoed through the cathedrals and chapels, a clarion call to restore the sanctity that revolution sought to erase. The sagacity of their responses underscored a profound commitment to the inviolable bond between heaven and the French faithful, striving to navigate the turbulent seas of change with an unyielding anchor of divine truth.

Efforts to Reassert Influence

Amidst the tumultuous waves of revolution that sought to drown the hierarchal sanctuaries within France, the ecclesiastical powers found themselves in dire need of reasserting their lost dominion. The sword of secularization had not merely threatened to sever their influence but had indeed struck deep wounds within the sacred body of the Church. The hierarchy—bishops, archbishops, and cardinals—saw no recourse but to muster their spiritual arsenals and relentless resolve, for the stakes were no less than the very soul of France itself.

In this time of upheaval, their efforts could not simply be a return to former glories. The landscape had irrevocably altered; the soil that once bore forth the fruits of faith now seemed parched by the sun of reason. Thus, the Church sought to navigate these new waters through a multifaceted approach—a tapestry woven with threads that were at once historical and innovative. These renewed endeavors found expression in reinvigorated liturgical practices, impassioned homilies, and most crucially, in the establishment of new forms of clerical and lay partnerships that aimed to restore faith among the disenchanted masses.

One of the foremost strategies employed by the hierarchy was the resurgence of catechetical instruction. Realizing the insidious effects of secular indoctrination, those in clerical robes deemed it necessary to focus mightily upon the youth. Religious education was emphasized not solely within the bounds of Sunday schooling but extended into daily life, where faith became an omnipresent sentinel guarding the hearts of the younger generation. Parochial schools multiplied even amidst the ashes of revolution, serving as refuges for a faith under siege.

Alongside educational efforts, the hierarchy knew the significance of reinstating traditional ecclesiastical ceremonies, which had been all but abolished during the Revolution's zenith. Festivities, processions, and the vigilant observance of feast days were reintroduced with a splendor meant to captivate the senses and light a fervor in the souls of the French populace. These ceremonials were rituals to reclaim the sanctity of time itself, to bind once again the threads of the divine into the everyday livings of the faithful.

The role of the printed word could not be underestimated. Recognizing this, the Church disseminated a barrage of pamphlets, encyclicals, and pastoral letters. These documents rearticulated the theological underpinnings of their faith, responding to the revolutionary narratives that sought to paint the Church as an antiquated, oppressive force. Epistles and treatises sought to illuminate the history of the Church's benevolence, its sacrosanct service to society, and its role as a moral compass throughout the ages.

The clergy, meanwhile, found their pulpits transformed into battlements from which spiritual warfare was waged. Sermons grew potent with purpose, emboldened by an urgency to reanimate the dormant spirits of their congregations. Preachers became warriors of the word, striving to reclaim the lost territories of the heart with every impassioned plea and fervent prayer offered from on high.

Intriguingly, the Church's renewal efforts were not devoid of political interplay. Alliances were cautiously formed with factions sympathetic to their cause, navigating the perilous waters of collaboration while maintaining doctrinal integrity. Through these alignments, the Church aimed to enshrine its presence within the governance of the emerging post-revolutionary order. The ultimate manifestation of this delicate dance came in the form of the Concordat of 1801, where Napoleon Bonaparte himself acknowledged the indispensable role of the Church. This treaty, while not without its compromises, bestowed upon the ecclesiastical authorities a renewed platform from which to wield their influence.

Beneath this veneer of strategic alliances and public ceremonials lay the silent yet steadfast efforts within monastic walls. Monasteries became fortresses of prayer and contemplation, steadfast in their commitment to spiritual regeneration. Monks and nuns doubled their ascetic labors, seeking divine intercession for the fractured faith of their nation. The resurgence of contemplative orders added a mystical element to the Church's broader efforts, reminding the faithful of the transcendental dimension that surpasses temporal turmoils.

Concurrently, the Church's endeavors were not limited to high clergy and monastic orders alone. The hierarchy astutely recognized the importance of lay participation in this grand scheme of reasserting influence. Lay confraternities and sodalities were given renewed emphasis, drawing ordinary men and women into the fold of active ministry. These groups became grassroots movements, nurturing devotion and pietistic fervor within local communities. The efforts of the laity became a vital lifeline ensuring that the tendrils of faith extended far beyond the cathedral walls into the heart of French daily life.

What is most poignant about this extensive tapestry of efforts is the unyielding resolve that marked the hierarchy's response. The Church in France stood at a precipice, faced with annihilation or rebirth. The clerical leadership viewed their mission not just as a matter of retaining influence but as a divine mandate to safeguard the eternal truths entrusted to them. Even as the secular winds blew fierce and cold, they remained a bulwark, a bastion of hope and divine order.

As we traverse the annals of history, one can discern that the very essence of these efforts to reassert influence lay not merely in actions designed for temporal gains but in a fervent belief that guided them. This belief was rooted in the conviction that the Church was eternally intertwined with the identity of France, a beacon leading souls toward salvation. Thus, the reassertion of influence was not merely a strategic endeavor but an enduring testament to a faith that refused to be extinguished.

In the final reckoning, these efforts began to bear fruit. Slowly but perceptibly, the tides began to turn. The seeds of faith, once thought desolate, found renewed life. Parishes began to swell with congregants, shrines saw the return of pilgrims, and the sacraments once again became vital stations on the journey of life. Thus, with divine grace and persistent endeavor, the Church started to reclaim its place within the soul of France, a place it never truly relinquished, even amidst the stormiest days of revolution.

Official Church Declarations

Amidst the tumult that roiled the very foundations of France during the Revolution, the ecclesiastical authority did not remain silent. The Hierarchy of the Church, bearing the weight of centuries-old traditions and the fervent faith of millions, found itself compelled to issue a series of declarations. These declarations served not only as a bastion for the devout but also as a clarion call for order amidst chaos. What follows is an exploration of these edicts, their profound implications, and the reverberations they cast upon the land of France.

From the inception of the Revolution, the Church sought to clarify its moral and theological stance in response to the unfolding societal upheaval. The first major declaration, the "Quod Aliquid," sought to address the rampant secularization and the attempts to excise the sacred from the public square. Issued by the Congregation for the Doctrine of the Faith, this document lamented the erosion of religious observance and decried the secular philosophies that had taken root.

Such a stand was neither taken lightly nor without consequence. With the issuance of these decrees, the Church unveiled the theological framework that underpinned its vehement opposition to revolutionary ideologies. These declarations often invoked the sanctity of apostolic tradition, asserting that the Church's preservation was tantamount to the preservation of the divine order itself.

One cannot overlook the profound gravity with which the Church approached the "Regnans in Excelsis," a proclamation that emphasized the inviolability of religious freedom. Addressed to the faithful yet aimed at the ears of the revolutionary leaders, this declaration foregrounded the sanctity of worship and the right of every individual to seek divine grace without constraint from secular authorities. In a time when priests were torn from their altars and sacred relics desecrated, such proclamations were more than mere words; they were a rallying cry for a return to piety.

Yet, the declarations did not merely focus on defensive measures. The hierarchy also issued documents that encouraged pastoral care and resilience amongst the clergy and laity alike. One such document, the "Pastor Aeternus," urged the bishops to remain steadfast and shepherd their flocks with renewed vigor. This was a clarion call to faithfulness in ministry even when the Church's physical edifices were reduced to ruins, and its very existence seemed under siege.

In a display of formidable resolve, the "Cum ex Apostolatus Officio" was brought forth. This pronouncement aimed to protect ecclesiastical integrity by addressing the necessity of maintaining orthodoxy among the ranks of the clergy. In an era where oaths of loyalty to the revolutionary government threatened to subvert the Church's foundation, the declaration reiterated that any deviation from doctrinal purity was intolerable. Intriguingly, this document served both as a theological statement and a mechanism for policing clerical conduct.

Furthermore, the synodal decrees played an instrumental role in reaffirming the Church's stances. For instance, the "Council of Embrun" brought together ecclesiastical leaders who articulated a collective stance against the civil constitution of the clergy. By underscoring the importance of the sacraments and the hierarchical nature of the Church, these synodal decrees underscored unity and theological consistency, offering a counter-narrative to the fragmentation propagated by revolutionary forces.

An equally pivotal declaration, "Nostis et Nobiscum," was issued as an apostolic encyclical. This document provided a rich tapestry of theological insight, highlighting the moral consequences of revolutionary actions. It drew upon scriptural exegesis and patristic writings to condemn the anarchic tendencies of the era, while simultaneously offering hope through a return to divine law. It posited that true liberty could only be achieved through adherence to divine precepts, a perspective that sharply contrasted with the revolutionary rhetoric of secular freedom.

Equally dramatic was the pronouncement of the "Ad Salutem," a decree aimed at galvanizing the faithful during these perilous times. This missive called upon the clergy to not merely act as spiritual guides, but also as bulwarks against the insidious spread of atheistic doctrines. It argued for a revitalized evangelism, focusing not just on maintaining congregational numbers but on deepening the quality of faith amongst believers.

The "Magna Carta Ecclesiae," another formidable document issued by the Church, served as a comprehensive affirmation of the Church's divine mandate and its role in guiding the moral compass of society. It delineated the boundaries between secular authority and ecclesiastical jurisdiction, effectively seeking to reassert the Church's dominion in spiritual and, to an extent, temporal matters.

Despite the formidable opposition, the hierarchy remained unwavering. The enduring influence of these declarations cannot be overstated. Over time, they worked their way into the doctrinal veins of the Church, fortifying its resolve against other forms of ideological adversities that would emerge in the centuries forthwith.

Moreover, the ecclesiastical declarations were not confined to the realms of the divine; they had tangible impacts on the social fabric. Legislative measures, societal norms, and even cultural mores were influenced by these edicts. The Church's proclamations provided a moral framework that many adherents clung to amidst the swirling maelstrom of revolutionary ethos, offering both solace and a sense of direction.

Indeed, the legacy of these proclamations extended far beyond their immediate temporal sphere. They laid the groundwork for future theological discussions and ecclesiastical policies, influencing not only the French Church but also the wider Catholic communion. As such, these declarations remained a testament to the Church's enduring capacity to assert its voice and vision, even in the most turbulent of times.

Chapter 14: Revolution's Long-Term Effects

As the fervent flames of revolution dwindled, their embers, though faint, reshaped the very soul of France. The once mighty bastions of religious piety found themselves eroded, caught in a tempest of reform and secularization. Those who held the faith were now wandering amidst the ruins of a society forever altered, grappling with a newly forged identity. The laity's observances, intertwined with the rhythms of daily life, began to slacken as the old bonds between church and state deteriorated. Yet, amidst these conflagrations, new paradigms of devotion arose, and from the ashes sprouted fresh expressions of worship, endeavoring to harmonize age-old traditions with a modern ethos. Thus, the lingering aftershocks of revolution echoed through the corridors of time, continually redefining the essence of faith within the very heart of France.

Lasting Changes in French Society

The dawn of the French Revolution heralded seismic shifts within the very fabric of French society, irrevocably altering the contours of its social, political, and ecclesiastical domains. This tumultuous period did not merely stir the hearts of its participants but etched profound changes into the country's collective consciousness.

Before the Revolution, society was rigidly stratified, with the ancien régime's tiers in stark relief: the clergy, the nobility, and the burgeoning Third Estate. The Revolution, however, set about dismantling these traditional hierarchies, seeking to dissolve the entrenched privileges that conferred undue advantage upon the few at the expense of the many. Equality became the rallying cry, albeit an ideal often eluding full realization.

The secularization campaign was one of the foremost drivers of societal transformation. With the Church's unyielding grip on daily life loosening, citizens found themselves navigating a world where religious dogma no longer dictated every decision. The Church's vast landholdings were confiscated and repurposed, diminishing its economic dominance and its role as a social bedrock.

The ethos of fraternity burgeoned in the public sphere, where collective participation supplanted previous modes of individual subservience to ecclesial authority. Ostentatious manifestations of piety gave way to more communal expressions of civic virtue. Such shifts, enduring and deeply felt, emerged not without resistance but galvanized a newfound sense of unity among the people.

Education, once the province of the Church, underwent a radical overhaul. The state assumed control, championing a curriculum devoid of ecclesiastical oversight. Schools became cradles of secular thought, imbuing a generation with Enlightenment ideals and a rationalist perspective that eschewed previous theological constraints. This had an enduring impact on the collective mindset, fostering a populace more inclined toward scientific inquiry and skeptical of religious absolutism.

The transformation also reverberated within the legal framework of France. Civil authorities articulated new laws that reflected secular values, supplanting the canon law that had previously held sway. Marriage, divorce, and inheritance all came under the secular purview, underscoring the state's ascendancy over ecclesiastical courts. The Napoleonic Code, in particular, crystallized these changes in a legal codex that remains influential to this day.

The eradication of feudal privileges served as a catalyst for economic dynamism. Peasants, erstwhile serfs beholden to arable lords, suddenly found the liberty to own and cultivate land independently. This newfound autonomy not only improved livelihoods but knit a more cohesive social fabric, where wealth and opportunity were seen as attainable through merit rather than birthright.

However, the Church, though diminished, did not disappear into the annals of obsolescence. The Concordat of 1801 marked a rapprochement between the state and the Church, allowing the latter to regain some influence, albeit within a framework that acknowledged the superiority of civil law. This delicate balance persists, shaping the ever-evolving dance between secularism and spirituality in French society.

In the realm of art and culture, the Revolution precipitated an epoch of fervent creativity. Freed from the shackles of ecclesial censorship, artists and writers explored themes that reflected the human condition in its manifold complexities. This cultural efflorescence enriched societal discourse, fostering an environment where diverse viewpoints could flourish.

Yet, the social contract itself was renegotiated during this period. The notion of citizens' rights and responsibilities shifted from a divine mandate to a social agreement rooted in reason and common welfare. Activism and political participation became not merely permissible but essential for the health of the republic. A more engaged citizenry emerged, one that valued debate, dialogue, and democratic participation as civic duties.

Importantly, the Revolution instigated changes in gender roles and expectations. Women's contributions, both in the public arena and within the private sphere, garnered new recognition. Although full equality was yet to be achieved, the seeds of future feminist movements were undoubtedly sown during this epoch, as women demonstrated their capacity and demanded a voice in the unfolding national narrative.

The scars and accomplishments of the Revolution left an indelible mark on French society, echoing through generations. Like an inscribed tablet, the societal changes engendered by this epochal period imbued France with a pervasive sense of modernity and a relentless drive towards egalitarianism. Each subsequent generation has been both a torchbearer of this legacy and a critic, striving to perfect the promises of liberté, égalité, and fraternité.

In sum, the French Revolution's legacy manifests in myriad aspects of contemporary French society. The dismantling of clergy and nobility's dominance, the reformation of education, the radicalization of civil and legal frameworks, and the enrichment of cultural life collectively illustrate a society transformed and continuously evolving. As heirs to this revolutionary fervor, the people of France carry forward a tradition of questioning and reform, ensuring that the echoes of 1789 reverberate ever into the future.

Impact on Religious Practice

Lo! The reverberations of the French Revolution echoed deeply within the hallowed halls of Christendom, forever altering the rhythm of devotions and the sanctity of religious rites. With fervent and dramatic strokes, the Revolution, akin to a tempest, upended centuries of meticulously woven ecclesiastical tapestry, and the Church, which had long stood as an unwavering sentinel amidst the changing currents of time, faltered under the weight of secular encroachments.

The Revolution did not merely rattle the temporal foundations of the Church; it reached into the very heart of religious practice, echoing among the sermon-laden naves and cloistered abbeys. Verily, the legislative chronicles of this tumultuous period mark the onslaught on religious traditions, beginning with the Civil Constitution of the Clergy in 1790. By attempting to bring the Church under state control, the Revolution sought to sever the bonds that held sacred its autonomy and venerate governance. Herein lay the genesis of an upheaval that compelled clergy and laity alike to navigate a labyrinthine reality of divided loyalties and clandestine worship.

Imagine, if thou will, the visage of a devout French peasant, crestfallen, as the peals of Catholic bells dwindled in frequency. Churches, erstwhile bastions of communal life and spiritual solace, became arenas of desolation or, in some instances, were repurposed as banal stages for the revolutionary fervor to play out. The process of *déchristianisation*, thus begun, unfurled with a vigor that sent tremors across the land. Religious feasts, once preludes to joyous communal gatherings, stood eclipsed by the revolutionary calendar, replacing the sacred with the profane.

Alas, the clergy found themselves particularly stricken. Those who took the constitutional oath were branded *juring priests*, while their non-juring counterparts faced prosecution and exile. The schism within the priesthood rendered the pastoral care of the flock a monumental challenge, with clandestine sacraments becoming a requisite for unsullied devotion. Thus emerged the unsung heroes of the faith, itinerant priests who risked peril and persecution to maintain the lifeblood of sacramental grace.

Moreover, consider the impact on monastic life. The Revolution's zeal to dissolve religious orders struck at the marrow of contemplative existence. Monasteries and convents bore the brunt of this dissolution, their inhabitants cast into the maelstrom of secular society. Quaint chapels and serene cloisters, once imbued with daily Liturgical Hours, found their cadence disrupted, the reverberating chant of *Ora et Labora* replaced by the clamor of a nation in flux.

The changing landscape of religious practice also bore witness to a transformation in religious symbols and rites. Where once stood statues of saints and martyrs, emblematic of divine intercession and celestial kinship, there now emerged icons of revolutionary idols, parading human reason and secular virtue. The fervent adoration of relics gave way to a rationalist disdain, and the pious processions, hallmarks of communal faith, waned under the watchful eyes of newly-established revolutionary guards.

As tumultuous tides swept the land, the laity, like the clergy, embarked on a clandestine journey to safeguard their faith. The homes of fervent Catholics became sanctuaries for hidden altars, where vestiges of sacrosanct rites carried on in hushed reverence. Baptisms, communions, and the Final Unction, all morphed into vestiges of subtle resistance against the burgeoning secular sovereign.

Amid this tempest, the birth of the cult of the Supreme Being, christened by Robespierre, signified another profound shift. Forming part of the new civil religion, it sought to supplant Christianity with deism, entwining political dogma and religious undertones. The elaborate Festival of the Supreme Being, a spectacle of revolutionary pomp, stood in stark contrast to the simplicity and humility revered by Catholic traditions. The monumental rupture between the sacred and the secular thus grew ever more pronounced, drawing a dividing line that would reverberate through centuries.

Yet within the seed of adversity lies the flower of resilience. Despite the revolutionary maelstrom, glimmers of invincible faith persisted. The sacramental life of the Church, albeit drastically altered, remained a beacon for many. Secret masses in secluded homes, whispered prayers passed in covert gatherings, and the enduring veneration of saints clandestinely honored, all bespoke a defiant faith that refused to be extinguished. The martyrs of the Revolution, their blood shed in the name of relentless devotion, cast a long shadow, a poignant testament to the unbreakable tether between Heaven and Earth.

Thus, as the Revolution ground its way into the annals of history, it left in its wake a landscape markedly transformed. The enduring legacy of this period, often characterized by its steadfast secular agenda, propelled the Catholic Church into an epoch of reevaluation and adaptation. The sanctuaries eventually reclaimed, albeit under altered dispensations, bore witness to newfound challenges, and an ardent quest for revival. The Church, with divine tenacity, sought to regain its moorings, navigating the intertwined paths of spiritual renewal and societal re-engagement, thus embarking on a journey to reconcile its profound heritage with an altered temporal reality.

Perhaps, in the grand tapestry of divine providence, the trials and tribulations wrought by the French Revolution on religious practice served to purify the Church, re-forging its mission amidst the adversity. A crucible that, while testing faith and devotion, ultimately reflects the resilience inherent in the divine connection, whereby the light of sanctity, momentarily shrouded, emerges resplendent and undimmed.

Chapter 15: The Lay People's Role

In the veritable maelstrom that was the French Revolution, a cadre of determined lay people emerged, embodying steadfast faith and unyielding devotion. Unto this assembly, the mantle of spiritual guardianship fell, as priests and religious leaders found themselves beleaguered or incarcerated. Their hands grasped at the tattered remnants of church fabrics, and with fervor, they wove them anew into the daily lives of those whose hearts yearned for divine solace. This was not mere compliance with dogma but a reclamation of sanctity amidst the profane upheaval. Thus, grassroots religious movements burgeoned, not ordained by vestments but kindled by ordinary souls seeking to light the path through darkened times. As revolution's flame sought to consume the vestiges of tradition, the laity's resilient spirit enabled a clandestine continuity of rites, and in so doing, they inscribed their pivotal role in the ever-unfolding tapestry of the Faith of France. Effulgent in their quiet ministrations, these unsung patrons of piety wrought a silent revolution of their own, anchoring the sacred against the tempest of the secular.

Grassroots Religious Movements

As the storm clouds of revolution engulfed France, the sanctum of religion faced unprecedented turmoil. Amidst such upheavals, the role of the laypeople emerged as a crucial catalyst in both preserving and reviving the faith that was precariously teetering on the brink of obliteration. Those who bore no ecclesiastical title, yet whose hearts were fervent for God, ignited grassroots religious movements that breathed life into an embattled Church.

The French Revolution sought to secularize society, but in so doing, it inadvertently sparked a fervent religious awakening among the laity. These men and women, stripped of traditional religious authority, discovered within themselves reservoirs of devotion and resolve. Unconstrained by the formalities and hierarchies that once dominated the ecclesiastical landscape, they became the new torchbearers of faith. In cottages, fields, and marketplaces, they gathered in secret to pray, to protect sacred texts, and to keep the sacred flame alive.

These gatherings were spontaneous yet intricate, a subterranean network of worship that defied the revolutionary decrees. Often, clandestine meetings would occur under the veil of night, wherein the faithful would recite the rosary or sing hymns, their voices subdued but unwavering. Wooden crosses and rudimentary altars were erected within homes, turning humble abodes into sanctuaries of divine worship. Thus, in a period where religious symbols were razed and churches desecrated, the laypeople asserted their sanctified defiance.

Their actions were not mere acts of rebellion but grand allegories of faith, each clandestine meeting a chapter in a larger narrative of divine perseverance. With no formal cleric to guide them, the laity drew upon oral traditions and shared memories of holy rites. Each soul became a repository of sacred knowledge, an unwritten gospel that nourished the community's spiritual hunger.

Additionally, these grassroots movements were marked by emotional highs and lows, as fits of religious ecstasies were often interspersed with moments of acute despair. The vigour of communal prayer would, at times, be tempered by the sobering reality of persecution. Stories abound of secret congregants who, upon being discovered, faced dire repercussions, from public shaming to harsher punitive measures. Yet these tribulations served only to fortify their resolve, deepening the spiritual camaraderie among them.

Moreover, the grassroots movements were a mosaic of various Catholic practices, each region imbuing its unique customs into the collective worship. In some areas, Marian devotions gained heightened prominence, as the Virgin Mary symbolized solace and divine intercession. In others, patron saints of lost causes were invoked, encapsulating the palpable sense of desperation and faith. This variegated tapestry of piety enriched the broader ecclesial tradition, transforming each laity-led congregation into a unique node of spiritual resilience.

Indeed, these movements often found an unsuspecting ally in the agrarian landscape of rural France. Fields and forests turned into cathedrals of nature, where God's creation itself bore witness to the piety of the faithful. As priests were persecuted and churches desecrated, the natural world offered refuge and a canvas upon which spiritual expressions could flourish. The whisper of the wind in the trees, the rustling of leaves, and the distant hymn of a brook became anthems of divine presence, echoing the communal prayers of the oppressed.

Some villages became known as strongholds of resilient faith, where the laity's fervour thrived with even greater intensity. Tales would spread of miraculous occurrences during secret Masses, further solidifying the conviction that God had not abandoned His people. Every answered prayer, every narrowly averted capture was seen as a divine nod to their unwavering faithfulness, a silent but profound assertion that heaven itself was aligned with their earthly struggles.

In times where traditional channels of religious guidance had been systematically dismantled, charismatic figures emerged from among the laypeople themselves. These were not ordained priests but men and women whose lives emanated a palpable sanctity. Such individuals often became the nucleus around which these underground congregations formed. Their words carried the weight of divine inspiration; their very presence evoked an aura of holiness.

Inspired laymen and women penned religious tracts and clandestine letters, smuggled across regions, adding intellectual heft to the spiritual revival. These documents revived theological debates and provided the literate laity with the tools to defend their faith against revolutionary ideologies. Texts smuggled from neighbouring countries, where the Church still operated openly, provided additional spiritual sustenance. Thus, literacy became not just a secular tool but a sacred instrument, spreading the seeds of hope and doctrinal clarity.

The laity also played an instrumental role in preserving sacred artifacts and relics, often hiding them in barns, cellars, or even burying them in fields, awaiting the day when churches would once again reclaim their sanctity. These preserved artifacts became not just symbols of faith but tokens of the courage and dedication of ordinary Frenchmen. Stories of such daring acts of preservation would inspire future generations and solidify the laity's role as the unsung custodians of France's spiritual heritage.

Through these grassroots movements, a potent realization took root: the indomitable spirit of faith resided not within the towering cathedrals but within the hearts of the faithful. The revolutionary government's attempts to obliterate religious practice, in many ways, only served to illuminate the laypeople's profound connection to their beliefs. As time weathered on, it became increasingly clear that the Church's survival hinged less on its hierarchical structure and more on the ordinary men and women who dared to believe, to preserve, and to worship amidst harrowing adversity.

When the clouds of revolution finally receded, the ecclesiastical hierarchy found itself turning to these very grassroot movements as sources of renewal. The post-revolution restoration of the Church leaned heavily on the regained fervour and the revived traditions that had been kept alive by the laity. The Church itself had undergone a transformation, now more acutely aware of the power and potential of its lay devotees. Henceforth, the relationship between the clergy and the laity was to be one of mutual respect and interdependence, shaped indelibly by the crucible of revolution and resilience.

Ultimately, the history of grassroots religious movements during the French Revolution stands as a solemn testament to the unquenchable spirit of faith. It serves as an enduring reminder that when institutions falter and authorities fail, it is often the seemingly ordinary individuals, touched by the divine, who become the extraordinary bearers of truth and light. In the intricate, tumultuous narrative of France's religious history, these lay movements are not mere footnotes but integral chapters, illuminating the path from despair to hope, from devastation to revival.

Laity and Revolution

As the shadows of disquietude and tumult did rise over the sacred land of France, a transformation unlike any other took root. The common folk, the laity, who once ambled in the serene light of ecclesiastical guidance, found themselves in the midst of an upheaval that sought to rend apart the fabrics of faith and societal order. Amongst these humble souls, the Revolution did not merely come as a foreign specter; it invaded their very hearths and hearts. To comprehend their role is to delve into a labyrinth of fervent faith and fervent struggle, of allegiance and rebellion, of resilience and capitulation.

The Revolution, with its clarion call for equality and fraternity, struck a chord in the hearts of many laypeople who had long felt marginalized by the rigid ecclesiastical hierarchy. The exalted vision of a republic, where liberty reigned supreme, spurred the laity to question the divine right of kings and the sanctified privilege of the clergy. The inequities that festered beneath the grandeur of the Church's monolithic edifice were no longer to be borne in silence. This awakening, however, did not strip the sacred from their lives. Rather, it sought to redefine it, to reconcile the sacred with the democratic ethos that was blooming with renewed vigor.

In the small villages and the bustling towns, the laypeople began to form societies and clubs, spaces where revolutionary ideas were discussed with as much fervor as were matters of faith. These assemblies, seemingly innocuous at first, soon became the crucibles where faith and revolution intermingled. Here, in the candor of evening gatherings and the earnest baptisms of newborn ideas, the laity's role metamorphosed. They became the torchbearers of a new vision, one that did not wholly forsake the Church but sought to wrest it from the clutches of corruption and avarice.

Even so, the path was fraught with contradictions and perils. The fervent advocation for secularization did not sit well with every heart. Many among the laity found themselves in a relentless tug-of-war, torn between their allegiance to the Revolution and their devotion to the Church. This inner conflict manifested in manifold ways. Some sought refuge in clandestine masses, away from the prying eyes of the revolutionary fervor that had begun to cast the Church in shadows of suspicion and disdain. Others, with a fiery zeal, took upon themselves the mantle of reformers, seeking to purge the ecclesiastical order from within.

It was during these times that the laity demonstrated remarkable ingenuity and courage. The making of clandestine chapels in hidden corners and the smuggling of priests for secret sacraments became acts of defiance and devotion. These are not just tales of rebellion but of a deep-rooted connection to a faith that neither the guillotine nor the Enlightenment could sever. The Revolution sought to dismantle the old order, but within this upheaval, the laity found ways to hold fast to their spiritual moorings, embedding the sacred within the very folds of their revolutionary fabric.

The relationship between the laity and the Revolution was also colored by the economic grievances that had long plagued the common folk. With tithes and feudal dues weighing heavily upon their meager means, the Revolution presented an unprecedented opportunity to break free from the economic stranglehold of the Church. The confiscation of Church lands, driven by revolutionary decrees, was met with a mixture of relief and consternation. While it alleviated immediate financial burdens, it also severed centuries-old ties to the spiritual landscape that these lands represented. The laity, thus, found themselves navigating a delicate balance, wielding the Revolution's sword yet mourning the loss of their sacred spaces.

Amidst this turmoil, the laity also played a crucial role in preserving the cultural and spiritual heritage of the Church. It was they who, in the hushed silence of their homes, kept the traditions and rituals alive. The celebration of feasts, the telling of biblical stories, and the preservation of religious artifacts were all undertaken with a reverence that defied the secular momentum of the times. The laypeople became the custodians of a faith that had been ostensibly driven underground but continued to thrive in the sanctity of their domestic lives.

Yet, the Revolution was not solely a narrative of division and conflict for the laity. It provided an impetus for a more egalitarian expression of faith, where the laity could assert their religious identity without the mediating authority of a decadent clergy. The nascent republican ideals permeated their understanding of faith, fostering a sense of personal responsibility and communal worship. Lay-driven religious movements began to surface, imbued with the spirit of the Revolution yet rooted in the timeless principles of Christianity. These movements often operated in parallel with, or in opposition to, the official Church, creating a dynamic and multifaceted religious landscape.

In this crucible of transformation, the laity's role evolved, reflecting their aspirations and anxieties. The Revolution, with all its chaos and uncertainty, presented a clarion call to re-examine and redefine their relationship with the divine and the temporal. While many embraced the secular ideals with fervent enthusiasm, others sought a path of reconciliation, yearning for a synthesis that could harmonize their revolutionary zeal with their undying faith. The laity's journey through the Revolution is a tapestry woven with threads of hope, despair, courage, and devotion, reflecting the indomitable spirit of a people striving to find their place in a rapidly changing world.

The Revolution, therefore, was not merely an external force shaping the lives of the laypeople, but a transformative epoch that provoked profound introspection and action. It engendered a religious reawakening among the laity, compelling them to forge new paths in their spiritual quest. The laypeople, amidst the storm of revolution, emerged not as passive recipients of change but as active participants in the remaking of their religious and societal landscape. Their role in the Revolution is a testament to their resilience and an enduring faith that, even when faced with the fiercest of tempests, found ways to prevail.

Chapter 16: American and French Comparisons

Contrasting the threads of the American and French revolutions reveals a tapestry of divergent paths where state and religion are interwoven. The American way, inspired by Enlightenment ideals and a pragmatic approach to governance, sought a separation that allowed faith to flourish freely without state intervention. Conversely, the French, amidst the fervor of their revolution, plunged into an abyss of secular zeal, vehemently uprooting the long-standing Church hegemony. The outcomes of these secularization efforts were striking; while America maintained a religiosity enriched by voluntary participation, France grappled with a profound spiritual crisis, the faith of its people shaken by the fierce de-Christianization campaigns. These differing approaches continue to echo through the ages, painting a complex picture of how revolutions can shape, and at times, scar the soul of nations.

differing approaches to religion and state

Verily, the American and French revolutions unfolded as epochs of immense consequence, wherein the destinies of religion and state tumbled through the annals of history in divergent manners. Each nation, with its unique ethos and cardinal precepts, embarked upon drastically differing crusades in defining the interplay between ecclesiastical edicts and the machinations of the state.

In the nascent American republic, an enduring harmony seemed to be struck betwixt the pulpit and the public square. The forefathers, in their sagacious wisdom, endeavored to reconcile the sacred rights of worship with the liberties of the civic sphere. Hence, they bequeathed a Constitution wherein the freedom of religion took pride of place, an unassailable fortress against the encroachments of tyranny. The First Amendment, much like a solemn oath, enshrined this liberty, foreclosing the establishment of any state religion whilst protecting the quiet sanctity of personal belief.

In stark contrast, the French Revolution, rife with the fervor of Enlightenment ideals, sought to unshackle the nation from the yoke of clerical dominion. The ancien régime had intertwined the altars of faith with the armchairs of power, to the point where disentanglement seemed an insurmountable endeavor. Indeed, the clergy's entrenchment in both spiritual and temporal affairs furnished a bulwark that the revolutionaries sought to dismantle.

This revolutionary zeal gave rise to the Civil Constitution of the Clergy in 1790, an audacious decree which sought to subsume the Church under secular authority. Priests and bishops were now to be elected by the citizenry and oath-bound to the state above the Holy See. Such impertinence led to widespread upheaval as many clergy, steadfast in their vows to Rome, vociferously resisted, thus sowing seeds of schism within the Church herself.

As the fervor of de-Christianization waxed and waned, iconoclasts dismantled the venerable symbols of faith — churches were repurposed, relics destroyed, and religious orders dissolved. The very heartbeat of the nation's soul seemed to falter, throbbing irregularly between the virtues of reason and the remnants of sacred tradition. The Convention's Calendar, stripped of its saints' days, mirrored the stark secular ethos now enshrined in law.

Meanwhile, on the western shores, America's approach appeared less tempestuous. Though the revolutionaries ardently sought to distance themselves from monarchical dictates, they did not endeavor to uproot the pillars of religious life. Rather, many colonies themselves had been sanctuaries for the persecuted and the dispossessed, fostering a spirit of religious pluralism that would become a linchpin of the American ethos. The separation of church and state, thus, wrought not a divide but a harmonious coexistence wherein each flourished within its own realm.

The differing histories of these revolutions, therefore, bespoke differing legacies: in America, an embracement of religious diversity under a secular aegis, and in France, a tumultuous break from clerical power, only to grapple again with the need for spiritual solace amidst the French ethos. And so, whilst the American revolutionaries enshrined religious freedom as the cornerstone of their new polity, the French revolutionaries embarked on a path of secularization that sought — sometimes violently — to reclaim public life from the grip of the Church.

The motives behind these disparate approaches lay not merely in political theory but also in the crucible of each nation's historical experiences. France's monarchy had a symbiotic relationship with the Church, each bolstering the other's dominion. The American colonies, conversely, were often havens for those fleeing religious oppression, fostering a landscape where multiple faiths could flourish side by side without state interference.

Thus, while the American experiment aimed to protect religious practice from governmental overreach, the French Revolution maneuvered to protect governance from religious overreach. Each path charted an odyssey through the tumultuous seas of human governance, steering toward different horizons, yet each seeking the shores of liberty, in its manifold expressions.

And so it is that the sacred and the secular, bound and unbound, have charted courses that elucidate the profound divergences of the American and French experiences. While America enshrined the coexistence of faith and freedom, France vacillated between de-Christianization and restoration, embodying a tumultuous spirit that reflected the nation's strife-torn journey through the annals of revolution.

In the eyes of history, and through the weighty lens of faith, each approach to religion and state offers a gordian knot of philosophical quandaries and practical discernments. France's penchant for secularism found itself at perpetual loggerheads with the tenacity of age-old traditions, whereas America's model flourished under the banner of freedom, where attended the lamp of religious pluralism alongside the flame of liberty.

Outcomes of Secularization Efforts

In the annals of history, the secularization efforts wrought by the French Revolution cast a profound and lingering shadow upon the realm of faith in France. The Revolution, a tempest of fervor and tumultuous change, sought to sever the intricate bonds that for centuries had tied the ecclesiastical to the civil, unweaving the very fabric of religious life. The aspirations of the revolutionaries to craft a society unshackled by clerical dominance and superstition bore disparate fruits in France and America, two lands embarked upon revolutionary quests, yet disparate in their visions of religion's place in the new order.

The French Revolution's fervent attempt at secularization encompassed a radical reordering of societal norms and mores, particularly in matters of faith. Envelop'd in the turmoil of de-Christianization campaigns, the French populace found their cherished cathedrals repurposed, altars desecrated, and sacred icons besmirched. The Constituent Assembly's Civil Constitution of the Clergy, in a sweeping decree, sought to subordinate the Church to the State, compelling clergy to swear fealty to the Constitution, an act viewed with abhorrence by many faithful souls. The resultant schism within the Church set neighbor against neighbor, rekindling ancient animosities and sowing seeds of distrust and division.

Across the Atlantic, the American experiment in secularization manifested differently. The fledgling republic, born of Enlightenment ideals and the valor of its revolutionary spirit, carven in its governance a wall of separation between the church and the state. Yet, it paid homage to the pluralism of religious expression. The First Amendment's eloquent respect for free exercise ensured a far different tapestry of spiritual life— a tapestry wherein clerical influence waned not by coercive might but by the natural progression of self-governance.

In France, secularization left an indelible mark upon the social and spiritual landscape. The relentless pursuit of laïcité sought to de-Christianize public life, to render religious observance a private affair, devoid of state endorsement or interference. Notre-Dame, venerated heart of Paris, was transformed into the Temple of Reason, symbolizing the Revolution's zeal to enthrone rationalism and cast out divine mysteries. The pull of secularization saw the abatement of religious fervor among the populace, with attendance at Mass dwindling and vocations to the priesthood suffering a dramatic decline.

Contrarily, in America, secularization engendered a context where religious diversity could flourish. The decoupling of church and state facilitated a milieu wherein faith communities could thrive devoid of governmental imposition, fostering a robust and variegated religious ecosystem. The dynamism of American spiritual life, unfettered by state dictates, contrasted starkly with the French secular rigor that sought to eviscerate religious institutions' societal influence altogether.

The ecclesiastical hierarchy in France, faced with unwavering revolutionary fervor, struggled to navigate these radical transformations. As abbeys and monasteries faced dissolution, and clerical lands were appropriated by the state, the Church confronted an existential crisis of unparalleled gravity. The Vendee, a region emblematic of the Church's resistance, became a crucible of rebellion, a testament to the lengths to which the faithful would go to safeguard their sacraments and sanctuaries. The bloodshed and strife of this counter-revolution epitomized the profound schism engendered by secularization efforts.

Moreover, secularization vehemently metamorphosed the Church's societal role. France's clergy, divested of their traditional privileges, found themselves thrust into a labyrinth of insecurity and marginalization. The public's distrust of the Church, fueled by revelations of clerical excesses and moral failings, exacerbated the erosion of ecclesiastical authority. In contrast, American clergymen, unencumbered by alignment with the state, engaged vigorously in the burgeoning civil society, becoming advocates for social causes and community leaders, thus reshaping their influence in a democratic context.

Yet, amidst the shadows cast by secularization, glimmers of resilience and renewal could be discerned. France's faithful, dislocated yet undeterred, sought new expressions of devotion. Underground networks of loyal clergy continued to minister to their flocks in clandestine chapels, defying revolutionary decrees. These unsung heroes of faith, through their enduring commitment, preserved the spiritual inheritance of France in the face of relentless secular onslaught.

Invariably, the outcomes of secularization efforts differed markedly between the two hemispheric revolutionaries. The French Revolution's systematic attempts at de-Christianization left deep scars, fostering an entrenched secularism that would influence French society for generations. The American approach, predicated on allowing faith to flourish free from state encroachment, resulted in a nuanced secularization that accommodated and even bolstered religious plurality. The French experience, with its draconian measures and resultant adversities, contrasted vividly with the American tapestry of religious freedom and innovation.

In reconciling the Revolution's secular legacy with the resurgent waves of faith that ebbed and flowed in its aftermath, one must acknowledge the indomitable spirit of the French Church. Though beleaguered and ostracized, it weathered the storm of secularization, steadfastly preserving its doctrinal and liturgical essence. The Revolutionary era, with its fervor and iconoclasm, imprinted a lasting impression upon French religiosity, yet could not obliterate the deep-rooted and ineffable connection between the French soul and its faith.

As we traverse the epochal chasm between those revolutionary days and our present era, we discern the enduring dichotomy wrought by secularization. It stands as both a cautionary tale and a beacon. The severing of entrenched clerical power from the state engendered freedoms and curbed excesses, yet also exposed the peril of disenchanting the public sphere entirely. The fabric of French society, woven anew in the crucible of the Revolution, would forever bear the imprints of its secular sojourn—imprints both luminous and lamented.

Thus, the secularization efforts of the French Revolution, an epoch of radical transformation, impute a legacy that endures in the collective consciousness of France. It is a legacy marked by paradoxes—a newfound liberty tempered by the reconfiguration of ecclesiastical power, a vibrant lay spirituality arising from state-imposed constraints. This comprehensive journey of secularization, with its labyrinthine consequences, remains pivotal to understanding the modern contours of French faith and its indelible crossroads with revolutionary secularism.

Chapter 17: Theology and Philosophy

The intricate weave of theology and philosophy amidst the throes of the French Revolution witnessed a profound metamorphosis, reverberating through the cathedral halls and cloistered minds alike. Canonical doctrines found themselves in a tumultuous dance with Enlightenment fervor, prompting a re-examination of faith's role within a rapidly changing society. The Church, long the steward of divine truths and moral compass, grappled with new intellectual currents that questioned the very bedrock of ancient dogmas. This era, bounding between fervent piety and nascent rationalism, saw French Catholicism adapt in script and spirit; while some theologians adopted a conciliatory stance, others entrenched themselves deeper into orthodoxy, creating a dynamic tension that reshaped doctrines. The revolution's upheaval spurred a renaissance in religious thought, one that challenged the faithful to discern and define their beliefs amidst an ever-evolving philosophical landscape, forever altering the visage of Catholicism in France.

Changes in Religious Thought

In the wake of the French Revolution, the landscape of religious thought in France experienced seismic shifts akin to the tectonic ruptures of old, which both forged new paths and ruined ancient strongholds. The sacred and the secular wrestled like Jacob and the angel, each seeking to claim the soul of France. This chapter shall explore the metamorphosis within the hearts and minds of the faithful, affected as they were by the winds of change that raged like a storm through the hallowed corridors of tradition.

At the outset, one must recount how the Revolution served as an anvil upon which new ideologies were hammered into form. The Enlightenment had seeded the land with notions of reason and liberty, which found fertile ground among the revolutionaries. This intellectual tempest tore through the Church's long-held doctrines like a scythe through ripe wheat, challenging orthodoxy with the fervor of the newly converted. The faithful, who once found solace in immutable truths, were suddenly cast into a maelstrom of doubt and reevaluation.

The dissolution of monastic orders and the secularization of ecclesiastical properties did more than just dispossess the physical domain of the Church. It ruptured the spiritual continuity of traditions that had been the bedrock of Catholic doctrine. Concepts such as the divine right of kings and the infallibility of the papacy were now rigorously scrutinized, their once unassailable citadels of thought assailed by revolutionary critiques. Faith was no longer a given but rather a question, an inquiry fraught with the peril of uncertainty and the promise of new understanding.

Within this ever-evolving theatre, a noticeable shift occurred in the theology of God's providence and sovereignty. The catastrophe of the Revolution seemed to many a test, a divine trial that demanded a rethinking of God's role in human affairs. The older theodicies, which presented suffering as a righteous path to divine reward, were now seen through the prism of revolutionary violence and estrangement. New, more existential interpretations of suffering and divine will began to emerge.

This epoch also witnessed an emergence of heterodox movements, each claiming insight into the divine mysteries befitting a nation reborn. Some sects returned to early Christian simplicity, eschewing the ornate dogmas developed over centuries. Others gravitated towards mysticism, seeking in visions and revelations what the tumultuous world denied them. The Church had effectively become a plural entity, its dogma fractured into many streams, each contributing to a broader, more inclusive understanding of the divine.

One must also observe the role of individual thinkers who, like solitary lighthouses amidst a tempestuous sea, cast their intellectual light far and wide. Figures such as the controversial Abbé Sieyès proffered notions that synthesized revolutionary principles with Christian ethics, positing that true faith could coexist harmoniously with the ideals of liberté, égalité, fraternité. These intellectual ventures expanded the boundaries of Catholic doctrine, daring to integrate the revolutionary spirit with the timeless teachings of Christ.

Furthermore, the very nature of scriptural interpretation underwent a profound transformation. The laity, empowered by revolutionary ideals, demanded direct access to the holy texts, circumventing the traditional clerical intermediaries. This democratization of scriptural engagement opened the floodgates to manifold interpretations, each tinted by the reader's revolutionary zeal or conservative restraint. The Bible, thus liberated, became a living document, dynamic and responsive to the individual's spiritual quest.

However, amidst the sea of change, certain islands of stability did remain. Traditionalists, often nurtured in the crucible of persecution, clung to the ancient forms with renewed fervor. Their piety was not merely resistance but a testament of survival, an unyielding stand against the tide of secularism. They embodied a faith that was both refuge and bulwark, defensively preserving the old orthodoxy while subtly adapting to survive in a hostile new world.

Moreover, the Revolution's impact on eschatological thought must not be underestimated. The upheavals of the period were seen by some as harbingers of the apocalypse, a divine reckoning for the sins of the ancien régime and the revolutionaries alike. This apocalyptic vision imbued religious practice with a sense of urgency and fervor, as believers considered themselves participants in a cosmic drama of salvation and damnation.

The sacraments, quintessential to Catholicism's mystical life, experienced both a diminishment in public practice and a deeper personal significance during clandestine observances. Baptisms, weddings, and mass were often conducted in secret, imbuing these rites with an aura of martyrdom and resistance. The persecution faced by the faithful added layers of meaning to these sacraments, transforming them into acts of defiance against the state's secular impositions.

One must not overlook the philosophical underpinnings birthed from the Revolution, which found their way into theological discussions. Existentialism gained a foothold, predicated on human freedom and the inherent responsibility of shaping one's destiny. Such thoughts resonated deeply within a populace disillusioned by institutional failure, prompting a reexamination of free will and divine foreknowledge. In this new light, the teachings of Augustine and Aquinas were revisited and reinterpreted to reconcile the tension between divine omniscience and human liberty.

The Church, battered but unyielding, sought to reassert its influence by engaging with these new currents of thought. Encyclicals and pastoral letters addressed the moral complexities born from the revolution, aiming to guide the faithful through the labyrinth of modernity. The ecclesiastical hierarchy embarked on a mission to synthesize the timeless tenets of the faith with contemporary ethical challenges, striving to present the Church as a relevant and vital moral compass in a rapidly changing world.

The Revolution also catalyzed dialogues between Catholicism and emerging sciences, fostering a cautious but meaningful engagement with scientific discoveries. Natural philosophy and theology, once entwined in a harmonious symbiosis, had experienced a fractious divorce during the Enlightenment. Now, in the aftermath of revolutionary fervor, theologians embarked on a reconciliation, seeking to demonstrate that faith and reason were not mutually exclusive but complementary pursuits of truth.

This era of theological introspection and growth was not achieved without cost. Many theologians and clergy, who dared to navigate the treacherous waters of doctrinal reform and intellectual openness, faced censure and exile. Yet, their endeavors laid the groundwork for a more resilient and adaptable Church, capable of confronting the challenges of a secular age with renewed vigor and confidence.

In summary, the French Revolution induced profound changes in religious thought, compelling a centuries-old institution towards introspection, adaptation, and growth. These transformations not only revitalized Catholic doctrine but also broadened the horizons of theological inquiry, enriching the tapestry of faith with new threads of intellectual and spiritual depth. The Church, having weathered the storm, emerged as a beacon of hope and moral clarity in an era defined by turmoil and transformation.

Impact on Catholic Doctrine

Embroiled in the convulsions of tumultuous upheavals, the French Revolution left nary a stone unturned. Its quaking reverberations permeated the very walls that upheld the Church, reshaping Catholic doctrine in ways profound and unexpected. As the ancien régime crumbled, the papal edicts and sacred scriptures bent under the force of societal transformation, as wood bends before flame. Theology itself was not immune; it encountered the stark glare of rational interrogation, a blade sharpened by the intellectual furies of the Enlightenment. Though the Gospel's eternal luminescence remained unscathed, the interpretations—the fabric through which the Church rendered its messages—began to shift like shadows at twilight.

To appreciate the weight and consequence of these doctrinal changes, one must consider the pre-revolutionary ecclesiastical structure. Grounded firmly in centuries of tradition, the Church held both temporal and spiritual sway. Catholic doctrine, untethered by modern scrutiny, thrived within an environment of relative intellectual complacency. The Revolution, then, broke forth like a thunderclap, shattering that environment and calling into question the unassailable truths long held by the faithful.

The Revolution's ferocity compelled the Church to reconsider its stance on authority and governance. The de-Christianization campaigns, suffused with vitriolic antipathy, necessitated a defense not just of theology but of the indispensable role of the Church in the foundational fabric of society. This conflict, in turn, precipitated critical introspections and, ultimately, clarifications and adjustments in doctrine. By reevaluating its alignment with temporal power, the Church sought to create anew its place within a reimagined political landscape.

One of the most notable shifts in Catholic doctrine was the rethinking of the sacerdotal hierarchy. The Revolution's inherent antagonism toward hierarchical structures, ecclesial and otherwise, necessitated the Church's reconsideration of its own. Papal supremacy, the episcopate, and even the role of the clergy were scrutinized under the revelatory light of egalitarian ideals. Though the Church resisted complete secularization, it could not entirely shut out the echoing cries for equality and justice that resonated from the Revolution's fervid heart.

Moreover, the sacramental theology faced its own set of challenges. As Revolution instilled in the populous a mistrust in longstanding institutions, the sacraments, too, were viewed with renewed skepticism. In an environment where reason was crowned king, the mystical essence of baptism, the Eucharist, and confirmation required creative apologetics. The Church found itself tasked with defending the transcendental in a corporeal-centric age. Thus, adjustments in catechesis and preaching ensued, aiming to bridge the chasm between an eschatological vision and temporal reality.

Consider also the revolutionary emphasis on individual rights and freedoms. Such ideals, while seemingly aligned with the Christian tenets of human dignity, forced an expansive rethinking of original sin and human nature's fallen state. While the Church maintained the necessity of divine grace and salvation, the manner in which these concepts were taught and understood began to see the inclusion of more dialogical engagement with those promoting Enlightenments ideals.

Significant, too, was the Revolution's impact on the Church's doctrine concerning the relationship between faith and reason. The Enlightenment, an intellectual precursor to revolutionary fervor, had already championed reason as the ultimate arbiter of truth. In the crucible of revolution, this perspective gained renewed vigor. The Church, which had long positioned faith and reason as harmonious partners, was now compelled to further clarify and defend this balance. Herein lay an immense undertaking: to demonstrate that faith was not antithetical to reason, but rather its culmination.

The doctrine of social justice also saw evolution. The myriad inequities that had sparked the Revolution led Catholic theology to emphasize more robustly the principles of justice, charity, and the common good. Post-revolutionary encyclicals began to address the socio-economic disparities laid bare by the Revolution's upheaval, marking a noticeable shift towards a more socially engaged doctrine. The Church, long a bastion of tradition, was now engaging contemporary social issues with newfound urgency and relevance.

Additionally, there was an introspective shift in the doctrine related to the moral authority of the Church. The misconduct and moral failings of the clergy, lamented and denounced during the Revolution, necessitated a doctrinal response to underscore the importance of virtue, integrity, and accountability among the clergy. Ecclesiastical documents and pastoral letters from this period reflect an increased emphasis on the need for moral rectitude and transparency within the Church.

The eschatological aspects of Catholic doctrine—those concerning the "last things" like death, judgment, heaven, and hell—were also revisited. The Revolution, with its assurances of a utopian society achieved through human effort, challenged the Church's vision of a divine culmination of history. Theologians of the time were prompted to assert with greater clarity the divine sovereignty over human history and the ultimate realization of God's kingdom not through human effort alone but through divine grace.

Lastly, consider the profound influence of the Revolution on the doctrine of religious liberty. The Church, which had traditionally embedded itself within the fabric of state structures, now faced a society gripped by secularism. This necessitated a nuanced understanding of the interplay between religious freedom and the public sphere. The Revolution impelled Catholic theologians to articulate a defense of religious freedom that respected the dignity of every person while upholding the role of the Church as a moral compass in public life.

Therefore, the French Revolution, with its avid repudiation of established norms, exerted a centrifugal force on the Church, compelling it to adapt, revise, and reassert its doctrinal truths in new and innovative ways. The Church, though scarred and wearied by the Revolution's de-Christianizing zeal, emerged with a revitalized sense of its mission and a clearer articulation of its age-old doctrines, now tempered by the fires of revolutionary change. The impact on Catholic doctrine was profound and enduring, a testament to the Church's resilience and its capacity to renew itself in the crucible of historical adversity.

Chapter 18: Military and Monastic Orders

As storm-clouds gathered o'er the land of France, and the revolution's fervent fire did threaten to consume all vestiges of the established order, the military and monastic brethren found themselves amid a maelstrom, their roles uprooted and their futures uncertain. The orders once sanctified by ancient rites and blessed by the annals of history were now caught in the crosshairs of upheaval and reform. The Templar-like defenders of the faith—those cloaked in the valor of chivalry and devotion—stood often beside, and sometimes in opposition to, their monastic counterparts, who, cloistered in contemplation, yearned for divine guidance. Conflicts and collisions of duty besieged them, creating a tableau rich in both valorous deeds and poignant disillusionment. As the revolution's tempest abated, the realignment of these orders under the new social and political paradigms marked both an end and a new beginning, knit into the very fabric of the post-revolution ecclesiastical tapestry. Their narratives echo through the gilded halls of sanctuaries and beneath the cobblestones of history, revealing a complex interplay of faith, duty, and transformation.

The Role of Religious Orders during the Conflict

The tempestuous winds of revolution, howling through the valleys and sacred halls of France, did not discriminate in their path of uproar. Amid this turmoil, the religious orders, both military and monastic, found themselves cast into roles both venerable and vexing. Their influence, though cloaked and oftentimes constrained by the very fabric of their vows, unfolded in tales of valor, subterfuge, and piety.

The dawn of conflict thrust the monastic orders into an existential conundrum. Steeped in traditions of charity, prayer, and learning, they now faced the dichotomy of loyalty to God versus subjugation to the revolutionary edicts. Within the ancient walls of their abbeys and priories, whispered debates on how to navigate the exigent demands of the revolutionary government filled the stone corridors. The sacred vows, inviolate before this upheaval, seemed fraught with peril when weighed against the decrees demanding allegiance to the nascent Republic.

Religious orders such as the Benedictines and the Cistercians endeavored to maintain their spiritual missions amidst the proscriptions laid upon them. Driven from their sanctuaries or forced into secular compliance, they waged a silent war against the erosion of their monastic life. Several monks and nuns, undeterred by the imminent threat of persecution, transformed their cloisters into refuges for those hunted by revolutionary fervor, their quiet acts of defiance serving as beacons of faith in a sea of apostasy.

More overtly, the military religious orders, whose origins were steeped in the tradition of holy chivalry, found themselves anachronisms in an age hell-bent on dismantling the old regimes. The Knights of Malta, the remnants of the Templar lineages, and other martial brethren who had pledged their swords to God and King, faced unparalleled trials. Their fiefdoms and fortresses, hallmarks of medieval piety and might, were appropriated or destroyed, their members often forced into exile or anonymity. Yet, a number among them continued to engage in covert operations, using their networks to protect clergy, transport religious artifacts to safety, and uphold the sacrosanct traditions of their orders.

In this maelstrom, the dedication to charitable works among religious orders did not waiver. The Daughters of Charity and the Sisters of Mercy, for instance, exemplified the enduring spirit of compassion. Even as state-sanctioned entities sought to supplant their influence, these sisters nurtured the sick, the orphaned, and the destitute, their ministrations often becoming acts of silent rebellion. In the quiet of night, in the hushed corners of hospitals or the concealed alcoves of chapels, their whispered prayers interwove with the murmurs of the afflicted, a sacred symphony defying the cacophony of revolution.

Allegory speaks volumes of the resilience of faith in times of tribulation. Consider the Carmelites of Compiègne, whose holy martyrdom became a testament to the indomitable spirit of the religious orders. Amidst the shadow of the guillotine, they ascended as lambs to the sacrifice, their hymn of the Veni Creator Spiritus the solemn antiphon countering the brutal finality of the blade. Their sacrifice ignited a fervor of sanctity that reverberated through the waning years of the Terror, a luminous instance of faith's zenith reached through suffering's nadir.

Though many monastic libraries fell silent, their treasured manuscripts confiscated or burnt, some orders undertook the monumental task of preserving knowledge. In secret and at great personal risk, monks and nuns copied texts, hid relics, and safeguarded the intellectual heritage of Christendom. This clandestine work ensured that despite the pervading darkness of upheaval, the light of learning and faith would endure, to eventually kindle anew in more clement times.

The religious orders also bore witness to poignant ironies. Whilst the revolution strove to unseat the traditions that buttressed their work, the very principles of liberty, equality, and fraternity resonated with the foundational tenets of many religious communities. Orders that had long practiced communal living, mutual aid, and devotion to service found ironic kinship with the secular ideals proclaimed by the revolution. Yet, this kinship remained unspoken and overshadowed by the enmity towards the institutional Church itself.

Post-revolution, the realignment of religious orders necessitated a restructuring of purpose and identity. The Napoleonic Concordat of 1801 sought to recalibrate the relationship between Church and State, offering a tenuous reprieve to the beleaguered religious orders. Nevertheless, the landscape had irrevocably shifted. Orders that once wielded considerable temporal power found themselves confined to spiritual sanctuaries, more reflective and perhaps more devout, their influence now a quieter force rippling beneath the currents of the new Republic.

Ultimately, the enduring legacy of the religious orders during this epoch of tumult is born of their unwavering commitment to faith and service amidst relentless tribulations. Whether through acts of hidden charity or overt defiance, their contributions illuminate the spiritual fortitude that sustained French Catholicism through its darkest hours. In their endeavors, the essence of their sacred vows—inviolate yet tested—served as a testament to the divine amidst the defiled.

Post-Revolution Realignment

The storm that was the French Revolution wrought not just terrors but also transformations across France, and in its wake, the Military and Monastic Orders found themselves in a landscape starkly altered. No longer could they stride forth in the old raiment of unquestioned authority and purpose. Instead, these religious sentinels, both martial and mendicant, had to navigate the tenuous and often treacherous paths between piety and practicality, between a past venerated and a future uncertain.

Post-revolutionary France did not swiftly unfurl a redemptive banner for these Orders. Rather, the rebuilding was methodical, rife with trials and tribulations, and a redefining of purpose. Military Orders, once wielders of righteous force, now had to refashion their martial fervor into something conducive to a nation reborn in the fires of egalité, liberté, and fraternité. Their swords, once instruments of divine justice, now faced obsolescence or repurposing in an age skeptical of both divine and royal mandates.

The path forward was one of prudence and patience. The Knights of older traditions found a need to adopt a garb less ostentatious, more attuned to the civic virtues now exalted by the Republic. Many Orders slowly shifted their focus from the battlefields to the burgeoning fields of social service, education, and healing. It became essential for these erstwhile warriors to don the mantles of teachers, healers, and custodians of communal welfare.

Monastic Orders, with their vows silently echoing in the ruins of their desecrated cloisters, sought to reclaim their sanctuaries and their sanctity. The post-revolution realignment demanded more than mere structural reconstructions; it required a spiritual renaissance. Monasteries found themselves in a dual role, serving both as centers for spiritual revival and as repositories of culture and knowledge jealously guarded against revolutionary iconoclasm.

Indeed, many monks, far from being mere relics of an anachronistic world, cast themselves as guardians of a timeless wisdom that transcended the immediate upheavals. They cherished the ancient manuscripts, the sacred chants, and the austere disciplines that had long defined their orders. Their relevance in a secularizing society was reaffirmed through a renewed commitment to humility and service.

Yet, this realignment was not without its casualties. Some Orders, unable or unwilling to adapt, withered on the vine, their glory days entombed within the annals of history. Others found refuge in foreign lands, scattering seeds of their tradition afar, where they might find more fertile ground for their spiritually rigorous callings. Thus, while the Revolution sought to sever the roots of monasticism, it only forced them to sprout anew in far-off places.

Institutions such as the Jesuits faced unprecedented challenges. Beseeched by both detractors and potential allies, they had to navigate a labyrinthine landscape of suspicion and embrace the roles of educators and reformers with measured zeal. The realignment drove them to refine their pedagogies and missions, aligning closer with the intellectual currents of the age while ever vigilant against encroachments on their doctrinal integrity.

The Hospitaller Orders, known for their care of the sick and infirm, became beacons of hope in a world ravaged by the very revolution that threatened to extinguish their existence. In a nation seeking stability, these Orders' steadfast dedication to healthcare and charity provided a nexus where revolutionary ideals and ecclesiastic virtues could coalesce. They embraced modern medical advancements, balancing them with age-old spiritual care, thus cementing their status as indispensable institutions in a rapidly evolving society.

With the concordat of 1801, a semblance of peace was brokered between the Church and state, yet it was far from a simple return to the past. The terms of this accord necessitated negotiation and compromise, reshaping the way in which Military and Monastic Orders could operate within the new framework. The post-revolutionary era demanded a rediscovery of relevance through a careful blending of tradition with innovation.

In the countryside, mendicant friars, once roaming with ease, faced edicts and laws that sought to curtail their itinerant lifestyle. Many settled into fixed abodes, establishing schools and orphanages that became pillars of communal life. These small pockets of piety and learning blossomed into oases of stability in a society still quaking from its revolutionary fervor.

The Benedictines, renowned for their ora et labora – prayer and work – ethos, amplified their engagement with agricultural reforms and scholastic efforts. Their self-sustaining communities served as exemplars of discipline and productivity, subtly advocating that faith and toil could together cultivate not just souls, but the very fields of France. Their abbeys, some reconstructed stone by stone, became symbols of Renaissance resilience.

Crucially, it wasn't only external forces that pushed for this realignment. The Orders themselves, deeply introspective, saw the Revolution as a divine alarm bell, calling forth a purification and re-dedication to their primal callings. This inward turn led to spiritual exercises that sought not only to reconcile with the temporal authorities but also to rekindle a fervor more focused on the essentials of their faith.

This post-revolutionary realignment, therefore, was not a mere adaptation; it was a renaissance akin to the spiritual awakenings of old. In weaving their old tapestries of divine service into the new societal fabric, Military and Monastic Orders showed that though kingdoms may fall, the soul's quest for divine harmony endures. Their tale in post-revolutionary France is one of reconciliation, renewal, and the relentless pursuit of spiritual valor, shown not in the clashing of swords but in the clasping of hands in prayer and solidarity.

Chapter 19: Economic Factors

The divine tapestry of France's socio-economic landscape was irrevocably altered by the tumult of Revolution, as gold and gall mingled in the crucible of change. Wealth, once held in sacred trust by the Holy Church, was seized and divulged amongst the progeny of Liberty and Equality. Churches that once stood as both spiritual and economic bastions found their coffers raided, lands confiscated, and their financial sinews laid bare. This unprecedented redistribution of wealth, driven by fervent revolutionary zeal, disrupted the ecclesiastical hierarchy, compelling the clergy to adapt to new economic realities. Thus, the celestial and the temporal intertwined, forging paths of suffering and salvation. The once intertwined fortunes of the Church and the state renegotiated their covenant, wrangling over sacred properties that once underpinned the very faith of France. The vaults of sanctity and commerce, long considered impregnable, yielded to the secular cataclysms, shrouding the future of ecclesiastical revenues in uncertainty.

Wealth Redistribution

To grasp the profound shifts brought forth by the French Revolution, one must delve deeply into the intricate web of wealth redistribution and its ramifications on the Faith of France. As the Revolution's throes reverberated through the cobblestone streets and ivy-covered monasteries, the reshuffling of material fortune commenced with an unprecedented fervor. This economic upheaval, marked by the transfer of assets from the sacred to the secular, played an integral role in shaping the religious and social fabric of the nation.

Prior to the Revolution, the Church held dominion over vast swathes of land and resources, enriching its coffers whilst enshrining itself as a formidable economic power. The sanctity of these holdings was fiercely guarded, underpinned by the belief that such wealth was a divine endowment, meant to uphold the sacred rites and charitable works that sustained the clergy and the faithful alike.

Yet, as the tempest of revolution gathered strength, the call for égalité resonated with vehement cries against ecclesiastic opulence. The revolutionaries eyed the Church's wealth as not merely superfluous but as a vestige of an inequitable ancient regime that necessitated dismantlement. Thus, the movement towards wealth redistribution was not merely economic but carried with it a potent ideological subtext, aiming to dethrone not just the monarchy but the spiritual aristocracy ensconced within the Church.

The Civil Constitution of the Clergy, enacted in 1790, struck at the very heart of ecclesiastical wealth. The decree mandated that Church lands be confiscated and sold off to benefit the nation-state, thereby diminishing the financial stronghold the Church once held. This legislative act was both dramatic and allegorical; a symbolic fracture as profound as any in the annals of history, where sacred land was wrested from holy custodians and thrust into the marketplace.

- Ecclesiastical estates were auctioned, often snapped up by bourgeois citizens eager to augment their own fortunes.
- The proceeds of these sales were supposed to alleviate the burgeoning national debt, yet they often found their way into the coffers of those already poised to exploit the upheaval.

The dismantling of monastic institutions exemplified this tumultuous shift. Monasteries, once bastions of both spiritual and economic stability, found themselves disbanded. Their treasures, amassed over centuries, were confiscated. The redistributive zeal of the revolutionaries saw these assets scattered, like seeds flung to the wind, profoundly altering the economic and spiritual landscape.

Herein lies the dramatic irony: As the wealth of the Church was dispersed, so too was its influence. The moral authority that had long been buttressed by material abundance waned conspicuously. This erosion of churchly power was not an incidental byproduct but a targeted outcome conceived in the revolutionary zeal to secularize society. Wealth, once a divine instrument, became a tool of political reformation and societal reordering.

The declericalized landscape also gave rise to novel challenges for the lay faithful. Bereft of the financial support once guaranteed by the Church, parishes struggled to maintain operations. Priests, once assured of sustenance through ecclesiastical revenue, found themselves in an unfamiliar struggle for survival. The confluence of faith and financial dependency was rent asunder, leaving behind a raw and fragile remnant of religious practice.

What, then, was the impact on the faithful of France? As the people of every hue and métier surveyed the newly leveled economic terrain, many felt a sense of disorientation and spiritual desolation. The intertwining of wealth and worship had bred a certain dependency, a rhythm of life calibrated to the Church's capacity to nourish both soul and body. With the economic foundation eroded, the faithful faced a vertiginous recalibration of their religious experience.

Among the broader societal implications of wealth redistribution was the rise of new forms of economic enterprise and class ascension. Those who capitalized on the redistributed wealth often found themselves in positions of power and influence, new arbiters of a society in transition. The emergent bourgeoisie, having acquired former ecclesiastical land and assets, embedded themselves in the new social order. For the Church, this signaled a profound alteration of its role: no longer an economic sovereign, it became relegated to a morally suzerain entity struggling to retain its relevance amidst a transformed class structure.

The drama of wealth redistribution was not confined to the halls of congress or the auction blocks alone. It seeped into the daily lives of the French populace, manifesting in both overt actions and subtle shifts. The transformation echoed in the echoes of village squares, in the hushed conversations of twilight gatherings, and in the private prayers of those grappling with the erosion of an age-old ecclesiastical assurance.

Ultimately, the spectacle of wealth redistribution serves as a poignant chapter in the larger narrative of the French Revolution—a chapter rife with allegorical richness, dramatic intensity, and profound repercussions. It laid bare the intricate relationship between material wealth and spiritual authority, delineating a path marked by upheaval and reformation. Within this turmoil, the fate of the French faith took on a new complexion, one that would indelibly shape the religious and societal contours of the nation.

Church Properties and Finances

The French Revolution, indeed, proved naught but cataclysmic for the realm of ecclesiastical wealth, wherein the resplendent properties of the Church fell victim to the sweeping tides of change. The opulent estates, which once stood as bastions of sanctity and abundance, teetered on the precipice of annihilation. The epoch heralded a radical redistribution of wealth, where the sanctimonious and secular realms collided in a crescendo of upheaval. With vehemence and fervor, the Revolutionaries sought to dismantle the affluent edifice upon which the Church's financial stability had been erected over centuries.

By an ambitious and audacious stroke, the National Assembly decreed the nationalization of Church properties in 1789. This mandate rendered all ecclesiastical estates and assets as property of the state. Vast swathes of land, cloisters, monasteries, abbeys, and churches, once sanctified ground, were commandeered and placed under secular authority. The largesse of the Church, which had been amassed over epochs, was thus upended, and with it, the influence that wealth conferred.

The revolutionaries, guided by Enlightenment ideals, perceived the Church's vast holdings as an anachronistic vestige of feudal society. They viewed the dissolution of these properties as a vital step towards establishing a more egalitarian societal structure. Yet, such appropriations were not executed without resistance. Clergy and laypeople alike found themselves embroiled in a maelstrom of contention, as the very foundation of ecclesiastical power crumbled beneath the seismic shifts of revolutionary fervor.

An emblematic figure of sagacity amidst this turmoil, Abbé Grégoire, sought to moderate the revolutionary zeal with prudence. His voice, though at times drowned in the cacophony of fervent discourse, called for a measured approach to ecclesiastical confiscations. His arguments underscored the necessity of preserving the Church's spiritual functions, even as its temporal powers dissipated. Yet, the whirlwind of revolution was not easily stilled, and myriad properties passed irrevocably into the hands of the secular authorities.

The fiscal ramifications of this expropriation were profound. The Church, heretofore reliant upon the income derived from its vast estates, now found its financial mechanisms shattered. This disintegration necessitated a recalibration of ecclesiastical finance. Tithes, those once-sacrosanct dues from the faithful, were abolished, leaving the Church bereft of a significant revenue stream. In their stead, the Civil Constitution of the Clergy attempted to reforge the relationship between the Church and the state, albeit with contentious results.

Within the boundaries of the ecclesiastical economy, this tumult yielded diverse outcomes. Seminarians and parishes, suddenly destitute, faced the grim realities of poverty. Monasteries and convents, stripped of their endowments, could scarcely sustain their inhabitants. The opulence that had once characterized ecclesiastical institutions was supplanted by a stark austerity. Yet, in this crucible of fiscal adversity, the Church's resilience manifested, as it sought novel avenues for sustaining its spiritual mission.

An auction of epic proportions ensued, as the biens nationaux—a term denoting the nationalized property—were sold off to the highest bidder. This fire-sale of the sacred yielded not only monetary gain for the nascent republic but transformed the socio-economic landscape. Lands that had once the solemn silence of monastic life gave way to the industrious hum of agrarian enterprise. The ecclesiastical patrimony, thus dispersed, entered into the annals of secular endeavor.

Nevertheless, the far-reaching consequences of these financial dislocations were not confined to immediate fiscal imbalances. The sinews that bound the Church to the rural fabric of French life were unknotted, setting in motion a cascade of socio-cultural reverberations. The patronage networks, which had entwined parish, peasant, and proprietor, dissolved, leaving an atomized rural populace adrift amidst the waves of revolutionary change.

As we traverse the narrative of this epoch, one cannot elide the tale of the non-juring priests, who, staunch in their refusal to swear allegiance to the

Civil Constitution of the Clergy, faced peril and persecution. These men of steadfast conviction were forced into the shadows, preaching in clandestine chapels and hidden sanctuaries. Their material destitution paralleled their spiritual struggle, as they navigated the twin threats of famine and apprehension.

In examining the financial reconstitution of the Church during the period, an intricate tapestry of resilience and adaptation emerges. Alms and donations, modest though they were, began to form the bulwark of ecclesiastical funding. The lay faithful, despite the burgeoning secularism, demonstrated their enduring commitment to their spiritual guardians by contributing what little they could spare. Thus, through the crucible of adversity, a renewed spirit of communal solidarity and support arose, an unanticipated boon amidst the desolation.

The revolutionary government, in its later stages, recognized the untenability of outright ecclesiastical destitution. The Concordat of 1801, a seminal treaty negotiated by Napoleon Bonaparte and Pope Pius VII, sought to ameliorate the rift and address the financial disarray. While the treaty did not restore the fulsome wealth lost, it provided a framework wherein the state assumed the responsibility for clerical salaries, thus ensuring a basic level of fiscal stability for the Church's operations.

Such arrangements, though pragmatic, were fraught with complexities. The delicate dance between ecclesiastical autonomy and state oversight introduced a novel dynamic in Church finances. No longer the unfettered steward of its vast assets, the Church had to navigate its financial stewardship within the confines of state supervision and support. This shift signified not merely a change in material terms but heralded a recalibration of ecclesiastical authority and independence.

Indeed, as we contemplate the enduring legacy of these transformations, it becomes evident that the revolution wrought a profound restructuring of the Church's socio-economic dimensions. The dissolution of Church properties and the ensuing financial recalibrations were emblematic of a broader ideological and structural shift. The ecclesiastical estate, once a pillar of ancien régime society, emerged from the revolution not unscathed, but undeniably transformed.

Thus, the annals of history reveal a saga rich in irony and resilience. The loss of material wealth, which at first glance appeared as a nadir, paradoxically engendered a renaissance of spiritual solidarity and communal support. From the crucible of revolutionary change, the Church of France, though stripped of its temporal wealth, emerged fortified in its spiritual mission, ever steadfast in its quest to bridge the divine and the terrestrial realms.

Chapter 20: Political Ramifications

In the wake of the tumultuous tides of revolution, the fabric of French society found itself irrevocably altered, leading to the monumental Concordat of 1801. This accord, like a masterstroke in the grand canvas of history, sought to redefine the once sacrosanct relationship betwixt Church and State. The Church, ravaged yet resilient, emerged from the ashes of subjugation to renegotiate its place within the reformed political sphere. No longer wielding the unchecked authority of yore, it now stood as a conciliatory force, aligning with Napoleon's pragmatic vision. The sanctuaries, erstwhile desecrated, found new purpose, balancing sanctity with the burgeoning ideals of a secular republic. The concordat, while offering a semblance of stability, beckoned the faithful to navigate a world where faith must harmonize with fresh civic duties, thus setting the stage for an enduring dualism within the heart of France.

The Concordat of 1801

In the tumultuous aftermath of the French Revolution, the relationship betwixt the Church and State was but a shadow of its former self, fraught with discord and mistrust. It is within this climate that the Concordat of 1801 emerged like a phoenix from the ashes, forging a semblance of harmony in a world torn asunder. This pact, promulgated by Napoleon Bonaparte in dialogue with Pope Pius VII, sought to reconcile the ravages dealt by revolutionary de-Christianization. A marriage of political shrewdness and ecclesiastical necessity, the Concordat endeavored to restore the spiritual fabric of France whilst bolstering the State's fortitude.

The political ramifications of this grand Concordat unfurled a cascade of significant shifts within French society, engendering a prudent reconciliation that mended the rift between devout Catholics and revolutionary republicans. Napoleon, ever the master strategist, perceived the utility of religious stability as a cornerstone for his fledgling regime. No longer would the Church be severed from the State; instead, a symbiotic relationship emerged, each entity entwined in a dance of mutual concession and benefit. This fusion heralded a paradigmatic shift that redefined the political landscape, influencing every stratum of the social hierarchy.

Foremost among these ramifications was the reestablishment of the Roman Catholic Church as a recognized institution within the French Republic. Though the Church did not reclaim its erstwhile supremacy, it attained a sanctioned presence, functioning with a degree of autonomy under the vigilant eye of the State. This newfound status accorded the Church a dual identity—both a spiritual haven and a tool of political influence. A delicate equilibrium was thus maintained, with Napoleon appointing bishops who would pledge their fealty to him despite their sacred ordination by the Pope. Such an arrangement ensured the continuity of clerical influence, albeit tempered by the omnipotent hand of the State.

The Concordat also entailed the restitution of certain Church properties, though full restitution was never within the realm of possibility. The revolutionary appropriation of ecclesiastical lands remained an indelible wound upon the Church's patrimony. However, the vestiges of what remained were deemed sufficient to reestablish diocesan structures and rekindle the flame of faith among the populace. The clergy, having endured ignominious incarceration and exile, found their ecclesiastical roles revitalized, albeit under stringent supervision. In essence, the Concordat reconstituted the Church's economic backbone, allowing it to function with renewed, albeit limited, vigor.

Yet, the Concordat's implications were not confined to mere structural reformation. It wielded a profound impact on the very psyche of the French citizenry. Emergent from a period of religious desolation and secular zeal, the populace gravitated towards the renewed religiosity sanctioned by the State. This accord effectively quashed radical secular fervor, replacing it with a tempered, controlled religiosity. The State, now arbiter and overseer of religious activity, ensured that faith became a conduit for patriotic unity rather than divisive zealotry. Thus, the Concordat fostered an ideological convergence that harmonized religious devotion with republican allegiance.

Indeed, the political ramifications extended further, into the realms of education and moral instruction. By reclaiming a measure of influence over educational institutions, the Church regained the capacity to impart moral and ethical teachings aligned with its doctrines. Schools, once arenas of secular indoctrination, now became venues for instilling virtues rooted in Catholic tradition. This restoration of moral authority significantly impacted the fabric of societal values, nurturing a populace imbued with a hybridized sense of civic and spiritual duty. It marked a renaissance of faith within the public sphere, imbuing daily life with a renewed sense of divine purpose.

Nevertheless, the Concordat was not without its detractors and limitations. The residual animosities from the Revolution lingered, manifesting in pockets of resistance among staunch secularists and fervent ultra-Catholics. For the former, any reconciliation with the Church represented a regression to pre-Revolutionary subjugation, whereas the latter decried the perceived dilution of ecclesiastical purity. Thus, the Concordat, though a masterstroke of political maneuvering, walked a precarious tightrope between opposing ideological factions. Its success hinged upon an ongoing negotiation of power dynamics, where neither the Church nor the State could claim absolute dominion.

This intricate balance of power was exemplified by the dual oaths of loyalty required from the clergy—first to the State and second to the Pope. Such an arrangement ensured a bifurcated allegiance, reflective of the complex interplay between secular governance and spiritual authority. Napoleon's astute political calculus dictated that while the Church could serve as an instrument of social cohesion, it must never ascend to a position of unchecked influence. The clergy, thus ensnared in a web of dual loyalties, became both the shepherds of faith and the guardians of republican ideals. This dichotomous role was emblematic of the broader political stratagem underpinning the Concordat.

Moreover, the Concordat of 1801 bore an indelible influence upon the broader European theatre. It heralded a precedent for the post-revolutionary reconciliation of Church and State across the continent. Other burgeoning republics, witnessing the French experiment, sought to emulate this model of harmony, albeit with varying degrees of success. The Concordat became a blueprint for subsequent concordats negotiated across Europe, shaping the contours of Church-State relations in an era marked by revolutionary change and social upheaval. Its legacy, thus, transcended the confines of France, imprinting itself upon the annals of European history.

In summation, the Concordat of 1801 was both a political and spiritual milestone in the reconstruction of post-revolutionary France. It symbolized the recalibration of Church-State dynamics, fostering an environment ripe for religious rejuvenation under the aegis of State oversight. While it did not restore the Church to its pre-revolutionary zenith, it laid the groundwork for a symbiotic relationship that would endure through subsequent epochs. The political ramifications of this accord were multifaceted, influencing ecclesiastical structures, societal values, and educational institutions, thereby charting a new course for the faith of France in the wake of revolutionary cataclysm.

Redefining Church-State Relations

Verily, the French Revolution, that tempest of fervent upheaval and societal transformation, didst not merely disrupt the monarchy but rent asunder the very fabric that intertwined the Holy Church with the State. As tidal waves reclaim the shore, so did the revolutionary zeal seek to purify and redefine a new order. The historic intertwining of the sacred and secular in France, symbolized by the close ties and mutual dependence between the Church and the monarchy, found itself under unprecedented scrutiny and assault.

In those fateful years, the Church, long perceived as a bulwark of the ancien régime, stood accused of myriad transgressions—its lands, wealth, and influence all marked for reallocation by the fervid architects of revolution. Ere long, secularization efforts took root, manifesting in legislative acts and societal decrees designed to cleave ecclesiastical authority from temporal power. The Civil Constitution of the Clergy of 1790 was both a harbinger and catalyst of this transformation, recasting bishops and priests as civil servants beholden to the Revolutionary Government rather than the Vatican.

The National Assembly, animated by Enlightenment ideals and a voracious appetite for reformation, compelled clergy to swear fealty to this civil constitution. Many a devout soul faced the agonizing choice between forsaking their spiritual vows and accepting the decree, or standing in defiance and courting martyrdom. This schismatic divide birthed a multitude of non-juring, or refractory, priests who held steadfast in their allegiance to the Holy See, a testament to the enduring reach of papal influence in defiance of temporal laws.

Concomitantly, the secularization initiatives extended into the very heart of ecclesiastical existence; monasteries and convents, those ancient sanctuaries of piety and learning, saw their venerable inhabitants expelled and their hallowed grounds repurposed for utilitarian ends. The once-sacrosanct churches were metamorphosed into "Temples of Reason," emblematic of the new civic religion fervently propagated by the revolutionaries, designed to supplant the traditional Catholic liturgies. Icons and relics, steeped in centuries of devotion, were shattered or seized, a dramatic and physical attempt to sever France's spiritual roots.

Amidst this backdrop of turmoil, one witnessed the dawn of a new and complex relationship between Church and State. As years passed and the revolutionary fervor evolved into varying degrees of reprisal and accommodation, it became clear that a complete extrication of the Church from the socio-political landscape of France was untenable. France, long the "eldest daughter of the Church," could not wholly sever its spiritual inheritance without profound existential repercussions.

In the ensuing years, with the ascent of Napoleon Bonaparte, the pendulum began its inexorable swing back toward conciliation. The Concordat of 1801, a landmark accord between Napoleon and Pope Pius VII, heralded a new era of cooperation that sought to reconcile the lessons and scars of recent years with the enduring need for spiritual governance. This accord, though restoring significant ecclesiastical properties and functions, encapsulated significant compromises as well. The state retained considerable control over appointments and the demarcation of dioceses, reflecting the enduring influence of revolutionary principles.

Thus, the Church found itself both restored and reshaped, a body simultaneously embracing its ancient tenets while navigating the turbulent currents of modern statecraft. The Concordat did not merely restore formal relations between the Holy See and the French state but rather set the stage for an intricate dance of power, influence, and negotiation that would define the future of ecclesiastical presence in the socio-political realm of France.

In the broader tableau, this recalibration of Church-State relations underscores a profound and lingering transformation. Never again would the Church wield temporal authority with the semblance of absolutism it once enjoyed. Instead, it would evolve into a spiritual institution operating within the carefully delineated confines of a secular state, its power mediated by, and in negotiation with, the apparatus of modern governance.

Additionally, this redefinition fostered a new sociopolitical landscape wherein the principles of secularism, or laïcité, would become deeply embedded in the French ethos. This secular framework, born from revolutionary zeal and tempered through pragmatic conciliation, signifies not merely the attenuation of ecclesiastical power but the genesis of a distinct national identity that places civic and civil virtues at the heart of public life. The echoes of this reconfigured relationship reverberate into contemporary France, where the balancing act between secular and spiritual continues to evolve dynamically.

Finally, through the lens of this epochal transformation, one perceives the profound capacity for renewal and adaptation inherent within both the institution of the Church and the broader societal fabric of France. The Church, though diminished in temporal terms, emerged with a renewed sense of purpose and mission, rededicated to its spiritual obligations amidst a rapidly changing world. This symbiotic reshaping speaks to the enduring resilience of faith amidst the crucible of revolution, a testament to the indelible mark left by this profound era of upheaval.

Such was the Revolution's indelible impression upon the sanctity and structure of Church-State relations that France's subsequent history would witness an ongoing and often turbulent negotiation of boundaries and roles. The narrative of reconciling faith with republican ideals, of spiritual authority within a secular state, stands henceforth as one of the eminent legacies of the revolutionary age, etching its lessons deep into the annals of French history and the collective consciousness of its people.

Chapter 21: Revival of Religious Practice

Thus it came to pass, in the aftermath of revolution's tempest, that a phoenix-like revival ensued in the fathomless bosom of France, where piety reawakened with fervent zeal. The air, once thick with secular decrees, now rang anew with hymns of devotion, as the soul-soothing bells of church towers tolled with renewed hope. Rebuilding that which had been razed, the faithful sought solace and unity within the sanctum of religious communities, restoring not just structures but essence. Monastic walls, once prisoned and silenced, resonated with prayer and divine adoration, while the Eucharistic candle flickered amidst the faithful's ardent vows. This resurgence was not merely an aesthetic renaissance; nay, it surged as an embodiment of a nation's enduring spirit, intertwining the sacred fabric of faith with the resilient threads of its people's hearts. Thus, the revival heralded a profound reawakening, imbued with an earnest longing for spiritual gravitas, echoing through the annals of history with hope's eternal hymn.

Resurgence of Devotion

Out of the tumultuous ashes of revolution and secularism, there arose an unexpected blossom that none had dared to forecast—a resurgence of devotion among the faithful of France. This rekindling of piety, fervor, and longing for the divine emerged not merely as a reaction against the desecration of sacred spaces and the persecution of the clergy, but as a profound testament to the indomitable spirit of faith that the Revolution could not obliterate.

When the gales of secularization swept across the land, intent on eradicating every trace of religious influence, it seemed for a time that the spirit of pious reverence had been extinguished. The churches, stripped of their treasures, stood forlorn and desolate, echoing only the whispers of the past. Yet, what the revolutionaries had not reckoned with was the quiet, unyielding resolve of the common folk. Behind closed doors and in the secret corners of their hearts, they sheltered the embers of their belief, nourishing them with whispered prayers and clandestine masses.

The cessation of overt religious practice did not equate to a loss of faith; rather, it transmuted the faithful into torchbearers of an invisible flame. As the Revolution relinquished its grip and the Reign of Terror waned, hope dawned anew. Fear and suppression could no longer contain the divine yearning that lay dormant in the hearts of the people. The fervor that once coursed through cathedrals and chapels found a new life in the return to sacred sites, albeit cautiously at first, like timid deer emerging from the forest's edge.

Central to this revival were the gatherings of the laity, who in the absence of an unshackled clergy, took upon themselves the mantle of spiritual leadership. These grassroots movements, impelled by a profound hunger for the sacraments, breathed fresh life into neglected traditions. The rosary, the litany, and the novena regained their places as focal points of communal and familial devotion. Herein lay a robust fortitude as the faithful found solace and fortification in one another's company, sharing not just physical bread, but the spiritual bread of shared faith and determination.

Moreover, the veneration of saints and martyrs surged with renewed intensity. These hallowed figures, once relegated to the margins by revolutionary decrees but never truly forgotten, became beacons of hope and exemplars of steadfast devotion. Their stories, etched into the annals of time with blood and sacrifice, rekindled the zeal of worship that had been forcibly abated. Icons, relics, and statues, many of which had been hidden away or smuggled out of desecrated churches, reemerged as focal points of prayer and veneration. These tangible connections to the divine and the holy intercessors reignited the spiritual landscape, bestowing upon it new vigor and vitality.

Not to be underestimated was the role of the surviving clergy, now often viewed as martyrs themselves due to their steadfastness in the face of persecution. Emerging from prisons and hiding places, these pastoral caretakers not only resumed their roles but did so with a newfound sanctity and fortitude. The scars borne by these priests testified to the resilience of faith even under the cruellest of duress, and their presence provided a powerful catalyst for the blossoming of religious practice.

As the shackles of the Revolution fell away, the Christian calendar once more marked the rhythm of life in villages and towns. Celebrations of feast days, pilgrimages, and processions saw attendees in throngs. Especially poignant were the pilgrimages to places like Mount Saint Michel, which loomed as a symbol of unbroken sanctity amidst the ravages of temporal power. This phoenix-like emergence of devotion saw an intricate dance between the sacred and the societal, as religious life gradually reintegrated into the once-secularized fabric of everyday existence.

The architectural grandeur of the once-desecrated churches was another catalyst. Committees formed, initially to restore what had been defaced or destroyed and later to reclaim the churches for their original sacred purposes. Stone by stone, tile by tile, the faithful restored these edifices, their labor an act of devotion in itself. With each chapel rededicated, each altar reconsecrated, the sight and presence of these holy places invited the people to return not just out of habit but out of yearning for the divine.

Furthermore, the Resurrection of Marian devotion flourished in this period of revitalization. The Blessed Virgin, seen as a symbol of endurance and hope, became the focus of renewed worship. Shrines dedicated to Our Lady experienced an influx of pilgrims, their prayers intoned in fervent supplication and gratitude. At these gatherings, the faithful partook in shared sacramental life, thereby knitting the community tighter through the bonds of shared belief and devotion.

Equally significant was the impact on younger generations born in the wake of the Revolution. These children, though initially distanced from traditional religious structures, found themselves drawn into this wave of renewal. Catechism classes recommenced with vigor, Sunday schools filled with the laughter and wonder of young souls eager to learn the mysteries of their faith. The baton of devotion passed into eager hands, ensuring that the rekindled flame of faith would not dim but grow brighter with time.

This resurgence was mirrored in the literary and artistic realms as well. Poets and artists, inspired by the renewed religious fervor, channeled their talents to glorify God and saints. Sacred music once silenced by revolutionary edicts resounded anew within the hallowed walls of churches, lifting the spirits of those who gathered to worship. The revival of religious art, stained-glass windows, and frescoes breathed fresh life into previously forsaken sanctuaries, transforming them into vibrant centers of spiritual enrichment.

Even the skeptical could not deny the transformative power that this resurrection of devotion wielded. The church, once a silent witness to its own degradation, rose again, not just as an institution but as a living testament to the boundless resilience of faith. This revival, though burgeoning in defiance of past oppression, ultimately laid the groundwork for the Church's future growth and influence.

And thus, in a remarkable turn of providence, the faith of France, tested by the crucible of revolution, emerged purified and strengthened. This resurgence of devotion did not merely return to the status quo of pre-revolutionary times but heralded a renewed and dynamic vitality that would shape the spiritual landscape of France for generations to come. The legacy of this rebirth continues to be felt, a poignant reminder that true faith, though challenged by temporal powers, is a force that endures and prevails.

Rebuilding Religious Communities

In the wake of the Revolution, France lay as a man once ferocious now subdued, its religious landscape marred and its spiritual edifices abandoned and desecrated. But even the darkest nights must give way to dawn, and so it was that the embers of faith began to flicker anew amidst the ruins. The Church, though scarred, embarked upon a resurgent path, driven by a concerted effort to knit back together the spiritual tapestry of the nation. This revival was no simple task, yet it was spearheaded by resilient souls who recognized that the very essence of their identity was interwoven with their belief in the divine.

Those who had once sought refuge in the silence of monastic cells or the bustling sacristies of parish churches returned with renewed vigor, determined to reclaim sacred spaces and reestablish the senses of community that had been fractured by revolutionary zeal. Monastic orders, which had been disbanded and dispersed, sought to reforge their brotherhoods, rekindle scholarly pursuits, and reignite the flames of contemplative prayer. The task was Herculean, yet their faith imbued them with the strength of spirit necessary to rebuild. The grand abbeys and humble chapels, though some lay in ruins, began to resonate once more with the chanting of the Divine Office and the harmonious murmur of the faithful gathered in prayer.

The laity, too, played an indomitable role in this divine renaissance. They, whose faith had been tested by the fires of revolution and secularism, arose as pillars of the Church. From the burgeoning cities to the pastoral countrysides, families and individuals took upon themselves the mantle of spiritual custodianship. They organized clandestine gatherings for the celebration of the sacraments, at times risking life and limb to ensure the continuation of rites that had been cornerstone to their ancestors' faith. Secret altars were erected, remote farmhouses became improvised churches, and the Eucharist was celebrated once again, albeit in concealment from prying revolutionary eyes.

Parallel to this, new religious fraternities emerged, their missions often clandestine yet their impact profound. These groups nurtured the spiritual and temporal wellbeing of their communities, providing solace to the bereaved, aid to the poor, and education to the young. The reconstitution of these communities bore witness to a surge of spiritual fervor that permeated through all vanes of society, invigorating the heart of a nation that had grappled with the void left by its attempted de-christening.

One cannot overlook the enduring symbol of Mount Saint Michel in this context. As the tides that surrounded it ebbed and flowed, so too did the tides of faith. The ancient isle, having borne witness to both the sanctity of monastic life and the stark desolation of imprisonment, became a beacon for the reawakening. Pilgrims who had once been turned away returned, feet weary yet hearts aflame with zeal. Monks and clerics, embodiments of resilience, began anew the cycles of liturgical life within its storied walls. The church bells that had been silenced now tolled once more, calling the faithful from near and far to the Mount's sacred embrace.

A significant factor in the revival lay in the very structure of the Church's hierarchical bodies. Bishops, who had survived the throes of revolution, endeavored to knit the ecclesiastical fabric together. They convened councils, issued pastoral letters, and reestablished diocesan frameworks that sought to bind together the disjointed parishes and religious houses. Crucially, these leaders often harnessed the spirit of reconciliation, not seeking vengeance against those who had apostasized or succumbed to revolutionary pressure, but instead welcoming them back into the fold with magnanimity.

Moreover, the printed word became a potent instrument in this renewal. Religious books, pamphlets, and catechisms flooded the cities and villages, sowing seeds of renewal in the hearts and minds of the populace. Missions were undertaken by itinerant preachers, who walked the length and breadth of France, delivering stirring orations that rekindled hope and reinvigorated faith. These preachers, many of whom had themselves suffered persecution, spoke with a fervor born of suffering and redemption, compelling the masses to return, repent, and rebuild.

It was not merely in the physical rebuilding of churches and monasteries that this revival bore fruit, but in the revival of the sacraments themselves, most notably the Sacraments of Penance and the Eucharist. Confessionals, which had long stood empty, became once again sites of deep contrition and grace. The Eucharistic celebrations, previously fragmented and hidden, emerged into the public sphere with renewed solemnity and fervor, drawing forth the faithful who yearned for the transcendent in a world so recently mired in turmoil.

As part of this grand renaissance, religious festivals and processions that had been suppressed found their way back into the heart of public life. These events, steeped in tradition and rich in symbolic power, stirred the communal spirit and drew the people together. The flickering candles of vigil masses and the stately grandeur of Corpus Christi processions, with their hymns and banners, served to reconnect the faithful with their spiritual heritage and reaffirm the Church's indomitable presence in their daily lives.

The restoration also reached into the realm of education. Religious orders, having regrouped, took upon themselves the crucial task of educating the next generation. Monastic schools and parochial institutions reopened, providing not just knowledge but imbuing students with the principles of the Catholic faith. These efforts were not confined to the clergy alone; the laity were encouraged to take active roles, thus ensuring the faith was transmitted through familial as well as institutional lines.

The efforts to rebuild were not free from challenges. The environment in post-revolutionary France was one of cautious optimism but also of suspicious scrutiny. The spirit of secularism still held sway in many quarters, and the scars of revolution were far from healed. Yet, the Church, through its resilience and the steadfast faith of its adherents, managed to navigate these turbulent waters, slowly but surely restoring a semblance of spiritual normalcy to a landscape that had seen so much upheaval.

In conclusion, the journey to rebuild religious communities in post-revolutionary France was as arduous as it was transformative. It was a process that required not just the physical reconstruction of sacred spaces but also the invigorative restoration of communal faith. The convergence of clerical zeal, lay piety, and the unwavering commitment to spiritual renewal forged a new paradigm for religious life in France. In overcoming the draconian attempts at de-Christianization, the survival and subsequent flourishing of these religious communities stand as a testament to the indomitable spirit of faith and the enduring power of communal devotion.

Chapter 22: Education and Indoctrination

In the wake of Revolution's fervor, the domain of education became a battlefield where the soul of France was contested. The establishment, seeking to strip the Church of its ancient tutelage, wrested the schools from ecclesiastical hands, replacing catechisms with the catechisms of reason. The altars of learning, once sanctuaries of divine instruction, now bore the semblance of the Enlightenment's altar, etched with the doctrines of secular thought. Children, erstwhile nurtured in the faith, found themselves at the behest of a state eager to mold citizens over saints. The crucifix, erstwhile a fixture over the scholar's bench, succumbed to the secular aspirations of the new regime. Thus, in these hallowed halls where once echoes of "Our Father" circled, now resounded the stringent maxims of civic loyalty, an indoctrination as potent as the faith it sought to eclipse. Herein lies the irony, that in attempting to eradicate the sacred, the state birthed its own sanctum of dogma, one where freedom wore the shackles of conformity, and where the heart yearned silently for the God it had been taught to question.

Changes in Religious Education

Upon a pivotal axis did the realm of religious teaching pivot during the tempest of the French Revolution, wrenching the North Star of Catholic instruction from old steeples to newer cosmic bodies. Abandoning the ancient rituals of pious instruction, the Revolution cast its shadow upon the methods by which the flock were groomed for their celestial journey.

Prior to this tumultuous epoch, religious education had long been entrenched in a firmament built by clerical hands. The catechism, diligently transmitted through generations, functioned not simply as a repository of doctrinal knowledge but as a moral compass steering the faithful towards divine truths. Herein, cathedral schools and parish classrooms stood as sanctuaries of spiritual learning.

As the fires of revolution raged, however, these sanctuaries found their walls breached, the very essence of their teachings besmirched by the burgeoning waves of secular thought. The once revered schoolmasters, many among them clerics, saw their staffs splintered and their pedagogical domains usurped by republican ideals. It stands then to ponder, what transformation of divine instruction ensued?

The National Constituent Assembly, in its fervor to remold a nation, decreed the Civil Constitution of the Clergy in 1790, a pivotal ordinance that thrust clergy into the web of state control. Here, the rupture between Church and State widened as pastors, no longer divine emissaries alone, became civil functionaries sworn to the nation. This legislature had roots sunk deep into the soil of rationalism and egalitarianism, aimed to expedite the disintegration of the clerical monopoly on education.

Henceforward, the parochial catechisms found themselves replaced by curricula owing more to the Enlightenment than to Epistles. The schools, once fortresses of theological indoctrination, became fortresses of secular instruction, where reason supplanted revelation. In the mire of this great upheaval, religious education wrestled not only with its content but with its heart and soul. Schools, erstwhile resounding with hymns and prayers, echoed now with the speeches of orators who championed liberty, equality, fraternity—those muses of revolution.

Governmental exertions extended further, for the Arts of Statecraft recognized no bounds. A new cadre of schoolmasters, fully vested in republican virtues, replaced the defrocked educators. These men and women, steeped in Rousseau and Voltaire, strove to impart a cosmology where divine providence held little sway over human destiny. The crucifix thus faded from classrooms, supplanted by the tricolor, a new symbol of fealty.

The layfolk, no strangers to devout instruction, found themselves adrift in this turbulent sea. The peasant child, once accustomed to daily catechism lessons under the auspices of devout nuns, now faced secular texts that espoused the virtues of the citizenry over the celestial. Far from the parish schoolhouses, doctrines of humanism glanced off the vaulted foreheads of the young, laden with questions hitherto nestled in the cozy certainties of faith.

Yet, priests and loyalists sought to turn this tide, albeit clandestinely. In the hushed recesses of hidden chapels and the secretive embrace of private homes, the catechism reclaimed its sanctified voice. Stories abound of itinerant clergy travelling incognito, resurrecting the ancient liturgies under the very noses of Jacobin patrols. Such courage reaffirmed that the divine spark, though dimmed, was never extinguished.

Nor can we sniff at the ingenuity of these devoted instructors, who employed the very mechanisms of their oppression against their oppressors. In regions less scrutinized by revolutionary watchdogs, Sunday schools resurfaced as phoenixes of ancient pedagogy, blending secular lessons with cryptic theology, ensuring the faithful were never wholly bereft of their spiritual heritage.

Despite these valiant efforts, the future of religious education bore the imprint of its revolutionary shackles. A nation struggling with its own dichotomy of faith and reason began to show the first inklings of a more pluralistic ecclesiastical landscape. Schools endorsed by the state now meticulously erected a scaffolding upon which reasoned debate and scientific inquiry could reside without the looming shadow of doctrinal dogma.

By the dawn of the nineteenth century, the Napoleonic Concordat of 1801 emerged as a complex mestizo, a treaty uniting divided sovereignties yet further complicating the purification of religious education. Religious instruction re-entered the public domain but now entwined inexorably with the secular. The laity, wearied yet compliant, absorbed this amalgamated pedagogy, a blend no longer distinct but woven deeply into the fabric of a nation torn between heaven and earth.

In this perplexing matrix, none could deny that religious education had irrevocably altered, reflecting not only a changed France but a Church re-imagining its pedagogy. The calcified methods of old gave way, and from the rubble, sprang forth a more adaptive doctrine, one bodily existing in the throes of modernity while reaching eternally towards the sublime.

The legacy of this transformation is not lightly dismissed, as it propelled the Catholic Church to reassess its educational paradigms, its symbiotic relations with state apparatus, and its role in shaping the moral universe of future generations. With resolute wisdom, the hierarchy understood that education was not solely the transmission of knowledge but a veritable battle for the soul of the populace. The Revolution thus set ablaze a new epoch wherein the Church and its faithful would continually wrestle with the education's corporeal and ethereal attributes.

Yet if the annals of history imbue us with any wisdom, it is this: the cataclysms of the past propel us not into darkness but towards a horizon where gallant souls endeavor to reconcile the temporal and the eternal. Thus did religious education through its turbulent transformation emerge as the vanguard of an enduring faith, tenaciously guiding the believers of France through the maelstrom and onto divinely ordained paths anew.

Governmental Control over Schools

Upon the tumultuous seas of revolution, the somber tides of change swallowed much of France's educational landscape. The new republic, zealous and fervent, sought not merely to rend the old order but to reshape the very minds of its young. Thus began a systematic and highly calculated dominion of schools by the revolutionary government, eager to sew the seeds of its nascent ideologies.

Before the upheavals, education in France largely rested in the arms of the Church. Institutions of learning were intertwined with the doctrines and sacramental vows of educators, whose foremost mission was the inculcation of faith. Schools acted as bastions of Catholic teaching, their lessons echoing the divine truths that formed the backbone of French society. Yet with the dawn of revolution, this ecclesiastical influence faced unrelenting assault, casting a shadow over traditions long held sacred.

In the wake of this seismic shift, the government seized control, dismantling ecclesiastical schools and establishing a secular system. Nationalism and rationalism took precedence, relegating religion to the peripheries of educational discourse. This change wasn't born of mere spite but from a zealous belief in the ability to sculpt a new citizenry less beholden to the past and more attuned to the revolutionary spirit.

One must contemplate the radical curricula introduced under state supervision. The scriptures and catechisms were replaced by texts exalting the virtues of liberty, equality, and fraternity. History was rendered anew, portraying the ancien régime as a relic of tyranny, its faults meticulously cataloged to engender disdain and deterrence. The writers of this new canon strove to supplant the saints with secular heroes, whose humanist virtues and deeds were meant to inspire an allegiance to the republic over the Church.

The most dramatic effect of this shift was the transformation of teachers from catechists to civil servants. These new pedagogues, often products of the state's education reform themselves, were tasked with instilling in young minds a loyalty to the republic. Their training was rooted in reason, their methodologies stripped of mysticism, all in service of birthing a generation loyal to the ideals of the Revolution.

This period also saw the rise of the "écoles normales," institutions specifically designed to train teachers in the new secular ideologies. These schools were not merely academic in nature but were ideological incubators, shaping educators to perpetuate the new socio-political order. By crafting both the message and the messenger, the government firmly entrenched its control over the future and its narratives.

One must not overlook the parental plight in response to the government's encroachment. For many, the school was more than a place of learning; it was a sanctuary where children were nurtured in the faith. The deprivation of religious education stirred a cauldron of discontent among those who saw the spiritual development of their offspring as paramount. Conflicts arose, some subtle and others quite open, between the religious and the state-appointed educators.

In provinces far removed from the fervor of Paris, traditionalism clashed poignantly with the new doctrines. Families and local parishes sought clandestine means to preserve faith-based education, much like the clandestine masses held in defiance of the de-Christianization campaigns. These regional resistances underscored the profound tension between secular ambitions and entrenched religious traditions.

Nonetheless, the revolution held its course, and the entwinement of political doctrine with educational pursuits grew ever tighter. The schooling system became a crucible wherein future citizens were forged, their identities molded by the hand of the state. The indoctrination was not always explicit; in many cases, it was the selective shading of truths, the emphasis on some aspects of history over others, and the heroic portrayal of revolutionary ideals that slowly coaxed the youth into alignment.

One cannot neglect the subtle, yet powerful, control exercised through textbooks and teaching materials. These volumes were meticulously reviewed by government-appointed committees, charged with the task of expunging ecclesiastical influence. History was not just taught; it was rewritten. Geography stressed the contributions of French republicans, and literature celebrated the voices that sang of new, radical freedoms. The very ether in which children's minds matured was carefully regulated to ensure that only the fragrance of revolutionary ideals seeped through.

Amidst this control, an irony lingers. The intellectual fervor that the revolutionaries kindled sought to replace one form of dogma with another, often leaving little room for intellectual freedom. Substituting divine command with state mandate, the new educational regime wielded authority with a fervor reminiscent of the Church's yesteryears. The blank slates of children's minds became the canvas upon which the new government painted its vision.

This grand enterprise was not without its challenges and failings. The diversity of regions, the deeply ingrained faith of many communities, and the limited reach of central governance led to inconsistencies in implementation. While urban centers often succumbed to the new educational mandates, rural areas held stubbornly to their traditions, allowing remnants of religious instruction to persist in shadowy forms.

Howbeit, the legacy of this era's educational reforms cast long shadows over French society. By placing education under governmental control, the revolutionaries set a precedent that future regimes would follow—a centralization and secularization of education that would outlive the fervor of the revolutionary period itself. The landscape of French education was irrevocably altered, its contours reshaped by the hands of those who sought to remold not just institutions but the very soul of a nation.

As we navigate the intricate web of these historical transformations, we observe how education became both a battleground and a vessel for ideological currents. The strains and efforts to control learning reflect a broader struggle for the soul of France, a contest played out upon the fertile minds of the young. It was a colossal effort to redefine what it meant to be French, an endeavor where the state wielded the power of knowledge as its most potent tool.

This chapter in the annals of French history offers profound insights into the intersection of governance, education, and ideology. It reveals how deeply the roots of control and influence can penetrate when state authority and intellectual formation conjoin. The ripples of these changes continue to influence modern French education and the delicate balance between secular governance and religious tradition.

Chapter 23: Martyrs and Heroes

In the hallowed annals of France's tumultuous journey through revolution, tales of valor and sacrifice stand in stark relief. The Revolution, with its fervent call for liberty and irreverence for old structures, wrought profound challenges upon the sacred institution of the Church. Yet, from this crucible emerged luminous figures who, weaving their faith tightly with their patriotism, resisted the tidal wave of secular zeal. These martyrs, toiling under unjust incarcerations and families sundered by decrees of de-Christianization, held fast to the ancient creeds. Their undying devotion not only fortified the Church's spiritual bastion but also etched their names into the annals of beatification and canonization. Under the shadow of Mount Saint Michel, where echoes of sword-clad Saint Michael once reverberated, these heroes etched indelible marks, becoming eternal beacons of a faith embattled yet unyielding. Thus, the intertwining legacies of blood, spirit, and scripture crafted a rich tapestry of resistance that reverberates through the corridors of Catholic history, a testament to the enduring power of belief amidst upheaval.

Figures of Resistance

Amidst the fervent turmoil and revolutionary zeal that engulfed France, there emerged individuals whose resistance against the tides of secularization and de-Christianization shone as a beacon of steadfast faith. These figures, though often disparate in their backgrounds and motivations, shared a singular commitment to the preservation and resurgence of the Catholic ethos in France. Rooted in their faith, they stood vehemently against the encroaching forces that sought to dismantle a legacy of religious tradition.

One such resplendent figure was the Venerable Abbot Augustin de Lestrange. With a choir of monks, he fled the impending desecration, refusing to surrender their monastic sanctuary at La Trappe. Journeying into the rugged terrain of Switzerland, he established new monastic holds, ensuring the survival of the Trappist order. His indomitable spirit was a stark contrast to the chaos of the revolution, embodying an unwavering commitment to monastic life and divine servitude.

Similarly, the saintly Sister Marguerite Rutan stands enshrined in the annals of resistance. A Daughter of Charity, she stayed in Dax despite the foreboding clouds of persecution. Her unwavering dedication to the sick and impoverished rendered her a target for revolutionary authorities. Captured and condemned under dubious charges, her martyrdom in 1794 elevated her as a symbol of unyielding faith and selfless sacrifice—a paragon for those seeking solace in turbulent times.

The tale of Father Pierre-Adrien Toulorge, now a Blessed in the Church, intricately weaves the narrative of resistance with the dramatis personae who defied the revolution's edicts. Born in Normandy, he endured a sojourn in Jersey, yet he returned to France, driven by his pastoral duty to clandestinely minister to persecuted Catholics. Betrayed and subsequently executed, his life and death imprinted an indelible mark upon the ecclesiastical history of resistance.

As France raged with revolutionary ardor, it was not just the clergy but ordinary laypeople who rose to become the ramparts of faith. In the Vendée, a rural populace espoused arms to defend sacrosanct traditions. Comprising farmers and artisans, their rebellion was a collective anathema against the Convention's draconian decrees. Citing faith as their battle cry, they fought with tenacity, blending piety with a warrior's fervor. The martyrdom of thousands in this counter-revolution etched a tapestry interwoven with sacrifice and spiritual defiance.

The dauntless spirit of Marie-Louise Trichet, foundress of the Daughters of Wisdom, radiates through the corridors of resistance. With her steadfast courage, she confronted the anti-clerical sentiments head-on. Resisting exile and imprisonment, she and her sisters persevered in their mission of education and charity, embodying the essence of Christian love amidst adversity.

Interestingly, the ecclesiastic structure too had its share of luminary resisters. Cardinal Jean-Sifrein Maury, despite his temporal entanglements in revolutionary politics, was a fierce advocate for the Church in the National Assembly. His oratory might and vigorous defense of clergy rights carved a niche for religious rhetoric in the political theater, reinforcing the spiritual in the heart of revolution.

Figures like Jean-Baptiste Lacordaire emerged post-revolution, who, though not a direct sufferer of the initial revolutionary torments, played a crucial role in reviving the Dominican Order amidst France's anti-clerical culture. His eloquent preaching and literary prowess rekindled the embers of Catholic thought, radiating hope and invigorating a new religious fervor in a secular epoch.

In the realm of silent sufferance and conscientious objectors, the story of Blessed François-Joseph de La Rochefoucauld, the bishop of Beauvais, is invaluable. He safeguarded his diocese against the confiscatory and irreverent mandates, even as he faced house arrest and ultimate martyrdom. His example bolstered the resilience of many who persisted quietly, yet profoundly, in their faith.

The narratives of these resisters are not mere hagiographies or historic reminiscences; they are testaments to an enduring struggle. Amidst the shifting vicissitudes of the French Revolution, their legacies underscore a ceaseless assertion of sanctity over sacrilege, an undying fidelity to divine providence over transient political tumult. These figures stand as incontrovertible pillars of Catholic resistance, myriad in form but united in essence.

From the abbeys of Cîteaux to the bustling streets of Paris, this resistance spanned cloisters and homes alike. The courage of abbots, the fervent faith of nuns, and the collective defiance of laymen coalesced to form a bulwark against atheistic aggression. Enmeshed as they were in persecution, their stories illuminate a resilience that was both spiritual and palpable.

In rural sanctuaries and urban tenements, the faithful held fast. Rosaries clutched tightly, prayers whispered fervently, sacraments administered in hushed secrecy—all these threads of resistance wove the fabric of a counter-revolution. The faith that had stood for centuries amidst cathedrals and crusades now found its battleground within the hearts and homes of ordinary believers, fortified by the inspiration of these exemplary figures.

The French Revolution sought to quash the Church and its adherents amid its sweeping reforms. However, in the crucible of this conflict emerged heroes whose sacrifices and fortitudes bear enduring witness to the indissoluble link between faith and resistance. Their legacies permeate not just ecclesiastical chronicles but resonate through the historical consciousness of a nation that confronted, contended with, and eventually negotiated its sacred traditions amidst the clamor for change.

Thus, the figures of resistance, the martyrs, the unsung heroes, are not mere historic relics but eternal sentinels of the Catholic faith. They existed, they fought, they suffered, and through their lives, the Church found a renewed affirmation of its divine mission amidst revolutionary France's secular tempest. Their stories compel us to reflect upon adversity's capacity to kindle an undying flame of devotion, a testament to faith's unassailable power.

Canonizations and Beatifications

In the somber aftermath of the French Revolution, a time fraught with tyranny and steadfast valor, the sanctification of certain souls through canonizations and beatifications emerged as a spiritual balm, a testament to their unwavering faith amidst persecution. These rituals, both solemn and jubilant, bestowed upon the Catholic Church an opportunity to acknowledge the sacrificial deeds of its martyrs, transforming them into eternal heroes.

The path to canonization and beatification begins with an ardent investigation into the life and deeds of the individual. This scrutiny reveals the extraordinary virtue and steadfastness in their devotion, even as the world around them crumbled. The French Revolution, with its tempestuous winds of secular fervor, saw many such souls who embraced their faith as their ultimate shield and sword. These figures, who once walked the soiled streets and hollowed halls, now traversed the celestial realms, their mortal acts paving the way for divine veneration.

Within the sacred annals of Catholic history, numerous individuals bore witness to their faith during this tumultuous period. For instance, clergy members who faced incarceration at Mount Saint Michel or those who suffered under the gruesome de-Christianization campaigns became paragons of faith. Their lives, filled with both ecclesiastical virtues and human frailties, were meticulously documented, scrutinized, and held up as luminous beacons of martyrdom.

But these canonizations and beatifications extended beyond mere acknowledgment; they forged a tangible connection between the faithful departed and those who survived them. For the Catholic Church, these ceremonies weren't merely a nod to past piety but an active participation in the continuum of grace and faith. Through beatification, the Church affirmed that these martyrs had achieved a state of blessedness, interceding on behalf of the living.

Moreover, canonization, the ultimate recognition of sainthood, signified that these souls had not only lived lives of exemplary virtue but now enjoyed everlasting communion with the divine. These ceremonies inspired, comforted, and fortified the faithful, offering a poignant reminder that the Church, even in a deeply secularized world, remained a formidable bastion of spiritual fortitude. The beatification and canonization processes, therefore, served as both a reliquary and a rallying cry for those devoted to preserving the sanctity of their faith.

In the richly woven tapestry of martyrdom and heroism, certain figures stand prominent. The Carmelite nuns of Compiègne, for instance, whose serenity and courage in the face of the guillotine became emblematic of resistance imbued with divine grace, were eventually put forward for beatification. Their story is not merely one of tragic end but of an enduring testament to faith unshaken by mortal peril.

Beyond the individual narratives lies the collective sanctification of countless anonymous martyrs who, in their own quiet defiance, stood as bulwarks against the tide of secularism. Their beatifications, often proclaimed in ornate ceremonies, reminded the faithful that even the humblest soul could achieve divine favor through unwavering devotion and sacrifice.

This intricate process of beatifications and canonizations involved voluminous compilations of testimonies, relics, and miracles attributed to the potential saints. Every word spoken in their defense, every account of their miraculous intercessions were weighed with the gravitas the Church afforded to one stepping towards sainthood. Relatives, friends, and the entire community often played roles in bearing witness, thereby knitting a communal fabric of faith around the individual being examined.

Equally essential was the theological discourse that ensued from these sanctifications. The Catholic Church, through canonization, also affirmed its doctrines and principles, validating the lives of these martyrs as embodiments of divine teachings. The beatification and canonization ceremonies were, hence, not merely ecclesiastical events but theological affirmations that strengthened doctrinal adherence among the faithful.

The canonization of martyrs from the Revolutionary period had profound ramifications for the spiritual revival in France. Following years of persecution and suppression, the sanctification of these individuals instilled a renewed zeal within the Christian community. Parishes once desolate saw a resurgence in attendance, and the laity found renewed purpose and fervor in their religious practices. Beatifications, in particular, provided immediate recognition and veneration, serving as a lighthouse of hope for devout Catholics navigating through the moral and spiritual fog of post-revolutionary France.

Indeed, these beatifications and subsequent canonizations acted as instrumental events in the restoration of the Church's influence. They celebrated the lives of those who had paid the ultimate price for their religious fidelity, thereby reaffirming the indelible link between earthly sacrifice and heavenly reward. The recognition of these martyrs fostered an environment where faith, courage, and devotion could thrive even under the looming shadow of secular authority.

As this sacred segment of the Church's history unfolded, it also brought out the dramatic narratives that imbued the Canonizations and Beatifications with layers of emotional, spiritual, and historical significance. It was, after all, within the ornate halls of the Vatican and the humble local churches that the canonized and beatified not only found their place among the saints but also within the hearts of believers, past, and present.

The beatifications and canonizations post-French Revolution were more than mere ecclesiastical accolades. They represented a complex interplay of spirituality, history, and human courage, engraved onto the very soul of France. The martyrs and heroes who emerged grisly yet glorified from the Revolutionary flames provided a divine symmetry to the chaos and underscored the eternal verity that faith, when tested, brilliantly illumines the path to sanctity.

Thus, the canonizations and beatifications bestowed upon these valiant souls embellished the chronicles of faith with spiritual luminescence, presenting the Catholic Church as resplendent and resilient. Each beatification an invocation of divine grace; each canonization a hallowed testimony to faith's triumph over temporal adversities.

Chapter 24: Mount Saint Michel as a Pilgrim Site

Mount Saint Michel, now restored to its rightful sanctity, rises once more as a beacon of faith and devotion. Its storied spires and ancient walls, etched with the whispers of centuries, call to the hearts of pilgrims who seek solace and spiritual rejuvenation. In the wake of the French Revolution's tempest, this hallowed isle has shrugged off its chains of secular desolation and reclaimed its venerable role as a sacred haven. Amidst the ebb and flow of tides, the faithful are drawn to its shores, finding in its rugged beauty a testament to resilience and divine providence. Here, the vestiges of monastic life and the echoes of angelic intercession meld, offering both a glimpse into eternity and a refuge from the tumult of the world. Thus, Mount Saint Michel stands, a sentinel of sacramental grace, inviting all who wander to a closer communion with the celestial and the infinite.

Return to Religious Importance

Amidst the lingering shadows cast by the French Revolution, the sacred island of Mount Saint Michel began to stir with a renewed sense of religious fervor. This imperiled sanctuary, once tarnished by the profane grasp of secular ambition, started to echo anew with the whispers of devout prayers and the solemn steps of pilgrims. The edifice that once housed prisoners had transformed, as if by divine intercession, back into a citadel of faith and reverence.

The journey back to religious importance for Mount Saint Michel was neither swift nor unchallenged. It demanded an unwavering commitment from the faithful, a collective yearning to reclaim the spiritual refuge violently stripped from the Church by revolutionary zeal. The process of restoration was an act of penitential devotion, as much for the land as for the souls who sought solace within its holy precincts. Enthralled by its historical essence and spiritual gravitas, the laity and clergy alike embarked on a pilgrimage of rebirth, re-consecrating the isle as a beacon of divine wisdom and sanctity.

Initially, the scars of its secular abuse were profound and disheartening. The once resplendent abbey, a symbol of celestial aspirations, bore the marks of neglect and desecration. The sacred relics had been despoiled, and the solemn halls had echoed with the laments of incarcerated priests rather than the hymns of veneration. Yet, this desolation only fueled the resolve of the faithful. They saw in Mount Saint Michel not just the remnants of a bygone sanctity, but the promise of spiritual renewal.

As per the ecclesiastic decree, efforts to restore Mount Saint Michel commenced with fervor. Artisans and craftsmen, guided by divine inspiration, labored to mend the fractures inflicted upon this revered monument. Each chiseled stone, each rebuilt archway, and each restored mural was a testament to the collective piety and unyielding determination of a people yearning for spiritual restoration. The work was arduous, yet suffused with a sense of higher purpose, infusing every effort with the sanctity of a prayerful vigil.

Simultaneously, the clergy resumed their rightful place as spiritual guides within these hallowed walls. They came not just as ecclesiasts, but as shepherds of a flock scattered and wearied by the tumultuous winds of revolution. Their sermons intertwined tales of resilience with doctrines of faith, galvanizing a renewed veneration for Mount Saint Michel. Through their sacramental rites and devout practices, they breathed new life into the spiritual heart of the abbey, rendering it once more a focal point of divine communion.

There arose a resurgence in the pilgrimages, mirroring the fervor of ages past when Mount Saint Michel commanded the steps of countless devout seekers. Pilgrims from far and wide trailed the ancient paths leading to the mount, their souls burdened by worldly tribulations and yearning for divine intervention. Each step they took upon the cobbled ways was an act of penance and an invocation of grace, drawing them closer to the sanctity they sought amongst the spires and cloisters.

In this pilgrimage, there lay a profound symbolism. Just as the mount itself stood resilient against the tides and time, so too did the faith of those who sought sanctuary within its confines. They came to Mount Saint Michel to renew not just the stone and mortar, but the living faith that resided in their hearts. The spiritual resurgence of the mount mirrored their own revival, a restoration of faith that could withstand the ravages of adversity and secular encroachment.

With the passing of years, Mount Saint Michel's reputation as a sacred pilgrim site was indelibly reestablished. The stories of its regeneration became tales of inspiration, imbued with the miraculous and the divine. The mount itself stood as a paragon of spiritual resilience, its towering facades and serene cloisters offering a stark contrast to the tumultuous secular world beyond its shores.

This return to religious importance was not merely a physical or communal endeavor, but a profound spiritual journey. It was an allegory of redemption and renewal, a testament to the enduring power of faith amidst chaos. As the faithful restored the sanctity of Mount Saint Michel, they held close to their hearts the lessons learned from the Revolution's ravages—ever wary, ever vigilant, and ever faithful. The mount, standing steadfast against the encroaching tides, was emblematic of an unyielding faith that could surmount even the most formidable adversities.

Thus, Mount Saint Michel once more became a beacon, a sanctuary of spiritual aspiration and divine intercession. It embodied the tenacious spirit of the faithful, a resolute bastion against the forces of secularism that had sought its demise. As pilgrims ascended its winding paths, they carried with them the collective testament of a faith unbroken, a relentless devotion to the sacred, and an unshakable commitment to the spiritual legacy that Mount Saint Michel so profoundly represented.

Modern-Day Significance

From its firmament amidst the surging tides, Mount Saint Michel stands as a timeless sentinel, its turrets and spires piercing the heavens, thus casting a beacon of hope and divine connection. No longer a place of incarceration, it has been redeemed to its ancient purpose—a sanctuary for the weary pilgrim seeking peace, solace, and spiritual elevation. In an age where materialism often beclouds the spiritual realm, Mount Saint Michel offers a reclaimed heritage, bringing forth a convergence of history, faith, and restoration.

The modern-day significance of Mount Saint Michel as a pilgrim site thus cannot be overstated. The wearied souls who ascend its steep paths do so amidst a whirlwind of spiritual reawakening. It is here, at this revered site, where the threads of past martyrdom and contemporary devotion weave into a rich tapestry of sacred experience. Worshippers and historians alike stand in awe of its dual inheritance: a testament to the trials it withstood during the French Revolution and its indomitable spirit that endured thereafter.

Such divine magnificence is not without layers of meaning. The renewed influx of pilgrims serves as a poignant reminder of the Church's resilience against centuries of tribulation and secular endeavors. Here is where they find sanctuary, a return to roots; an echo of medieval piety that once saw tens of thousands trod the same paths in reverence. The pilgrimage is not merely an act of devotion but a pilgrimage back through time, into the heart of what it means to stand steadfast in one's faith.

In these hallowed corridors, faith and history intertwine in dramatic confluence. Indeed, many who find their way to Mount Saint Michel do so with a quest not unlike that of the ancient knights and clergy. The very walls that once confined the devout during the Revolution now release the spirit into the sacred air, an allegory of faith unchained. One can almost hear the whispered prayers of the past meld with the fervent petitions of today, making Mount Saint Michel an eternal altar in the body of France.

The sacred ritual of pilgrimage to Mount Saint Michel becomes a testament to the enduring strength of religious even amidst secular advances. It becomes a reckoning, a pastoral invocation towards the heavens that asserts faith's victory over adversity. The sepulchral shadows of Saint Michael's Abbey juxtapose the divine light illuminating the path of each pilgrim, casting an ethereal aura that palpates the soul.

Furthermore, the site has assumed a new role in an age dominated by digital expanse: that of a crossroads between ancient faith traditions and modern spirituality. Pilgrims equipped with camera phones and tablets capture not just images, but fractions of divinity that can be revisited and reflected upon. The sacred becomes accessible, acting as an antidote to an ever-increasingly fragmented spiritual life. It is within this digital relic-keeping that Mount Saint Michel finds its place in the collective conscience of the modern Catholic.

Yet, not all who approach Mount Saint Michel do so with religious inclinations; a great multitude consists of historians, architects, and the simply curious. For them, the pilgrimage is one towards enlightenment on the capabilities of medieval engineering and the manifestation of human tenacity through epochs of strife and serenity. The edifice offers a labyrinthine revelation of human mastery over both art and adversity, making the journey as much an educational endeavor as it is a spiritual odyssey.

The pilgrims' stories, replete with their myriad origins and purposes, create a symphony of human dignity, rich in its diversity. Thus, Mount Saint Michel retains its place as a sanctified convergence, embracing all who seek its fortified grace. Affectionately termed the 'Heaven's Castle in the Sea,' the holy mount embodies the hopes, dreams, and silent prayers of those who perceive it as more than just an architectural marvel, but as a living testament to the divine.

Moreover, the site itself has inspired literature, art, and philosophical rumination, making it not merely a religious stronghold but an epicenter of cultural reverence. Generations of artists have chronicled its grandeur in paintings, poems, and novels, imbuing each creation with the ethereal qualities inherent in the mount. These artistic endeavors serve as auxiliary forms of pilgrimage, bringing the enchantment of Mount Saint Michel to those unable to tread its sacred stones.

Attendance at the Mount's venerable masses has surged, and the sacramental rites performed within its ancient walls possess heightened meaning. Baptisms, weddings, and ordinations conducted in the shadow of its towering steeple bear a semblance to the initial intent of the mount—a divine union between heaven and earth. These ceremonies evoke the sense of continuity, further binding the present-day faithful to their ancestral lineage of believers.

Yet, beyond the ceremonious, the more silent vigils and personal moments of prayer mark the mount with an ineffable sacredness. Individuals lost in contemplation find that the spirit of Saint Michael, the great archangel, pervades their thoughts and reverberates through their hopes. It is within this personal and communal act of grace that Mount Saint Michel transcends its physical boundary to become a bastion of the divine.

Moreover, the depth of its modern-day significance is echoed by the various orders of monks and nuns who now inhabit the mount, embodying centuries of spiritual custodianship. Their chants and rituals offer a continuous living tradition, a line unbroken even by the tumult of the Revolution. Pilgrims, touched by this resilience, often find renewed faith, gazing upon the monastic devotion with a revived sense of purpose and calling.

Thus, Mount Saint Michel stands as a monumental testament to the tenacity of faith through the ages. It endures not just as a relic of past glory but as a rejuvenating force in the present, guiding all who seek its hallowed grounds. Its tides, ever-unyielding, mirror the constancy of God's grace —a force of nature and divinity combined, irresistible and irrevocable.

Current pilgrimages to Mount Saint Michel bear the hallmark of searching and yearning—attributes as ancient as humanity itself. Engraved in its timbers and stones is the legacy of faith, a canvas upon which countless narratives of devotion, sacrifice, and redemption have been inscribed. Here, Mount Saint Michel invites all to partake in its sacrament of transformation, an eternal call that endures through the epochs, whispering truths to those who dare ascend.

Chapter 25: France's Dual Identity

France, with the paradoxical nature of a chameleon, has perpetually oscillated between the realms of the spiritual and the secular. This land, once exuberant with fervent piety, transformed under the embers of revolution into a landscape of rampant secularism. On one hand, it is imbued with the deep-rooted vestiges of Catholicism, echoing through its cathedrals and sanctified relics; on the other, it fervently embraces the ideals of liberty, equality, and fraternity, often at the expense of its ecclesiastical heritage. This dual identity, provocative and resilient, generates an inexorable tension—a dance as old as the Revolution itself. The soul of France seems forever divided, a land where the cloister and the Enlightenment boulevard both vie for ascendancy, each symbolizing the nation's profound struggle to reconcile its sacred traditions with the unyielding march of secular modernity.

Secularism vs. Spirituality

Amid the echoes of the French Revolution, the struggle between secularism and spirituality began to define the very essence of France's dual identity. The Revolution unfurled a dramatic canvas where the fervor of secular ideology sought to eclipse the longstanding spiritual heritage deeply embedded within the nation's soul.

The Revolution, with its clarion call for liberty, equality, and fraternity, embraced secularism as a means to reshape French society. It aimed to dissolve the bonds that tethered the populace to the Church, envisioning a republic free from ecclesiastical influence. Yet, this secular resurgence did not arise in a vacuum; it was a reaction to centuries of clerical power and perceived corruption. Thus began an era where faith and reason, sanctity and skepticism, stood opposed in a grand, tumultuous narrative.

In this epoch, Mount Saint Michel remained a poignant symbol, reflecting this duality. Once a beacon of spiritual pilgrimage, the mount became a penitentiary during the Revolution, housing those who once shepherded souls. Its transformation mirrored the broader societal metamorphosis from sacred to secular, embodying both the retreat and resilience of faith. Spirituality did not vanish; it morphed, adapted, and often contested the encroachments of secularism.

Yet, the spirit of the French remained undecided, wavering between the allure of secular enlightenment and the comfort of enduring spiritual traditions. France's dual identity emerged, not as a binary opposition but a nuanced cohabitation of secular and spiritual realms. The populace, caught in this ideological maelstrom, often found solace in private faith if public worship was curtailed. The heart may stray, but it does not sever easily from its roots.

The Church, now facing the brunt of secular zeal, found its influence waning but not extinguished. The Revolution's de-Christianization campaigns aimed to secularize time itself, replacing the Gregorian calendar with the Revolutionary one, eradicating religious symbolism from everyday life. Jean-Baptiste Carrier, one of the Revolution's most ardent secularists, epitomized this fervor by persecuting the clergy in a bid to cleanse France of its spiritual bonds.

In contrast, spirituality demonstrated resilience. It survived in whispered prayers, secret masses, and clandestine gatherings. The faithful, now scattered and subdued, held on to their beliefs with tenacity. They turned to relics, family traditions, and personal piety, fostering an undercurrent of spirituality that resisted being silenced. This tension between secular impositions and spiritual resilience lent a dramatic intensity to France's national character, forging an identity that oscillated between the temporal and the eternal.

France's Enlightenment thinkers, including Voltaire and Rousseau, had set the intellectual stage for secularism, questioning the Church's moral and intellectual authority. They envisioned a society governed by reason, where human rights prevailed over divine mandates. The fruits of this Enlightenment thought found fertile ground during the Revolution, leading to the proliferation of deistic and atheistic ideologies.

Conversely, the aftermath of the Revolution did not obliterate spirituality but restructured it. The Concordat of 1801, although primarily a political arrangement, underscored the necessity of reconciling secular governance with spiritual needs. Napoleon Bonaparte recognized that the soul of France could not thrive on secular principles alone. Thus, the Concordat reintroduced the Church, albeit in a new guise, into the fabric of French society, paving the way for a more subdued yet persistent coexistence between secularism and spirituality.

Moreover, the Revolution's disdain for monastic orders reflected its broader secular agenda. Monasteries, once the bastions of spiritual life and scholarly pursuit, were dismantled, their inhabitants dispersed. Yet, many monks and nuns continued their vocations in secrecy, preserving spiritual wisdom and practice even in exile. Such perseverance exemplified the enduring spirit of spirituality amidst secular oppression.

France's dual identity, rooted in both secular critique and spiritual continuity, shaped its cultural and intellectual progress. Literature, art, and philosophy flourished in this complex dynamic, often reflecting and commenting on the ongoing tensions. The juxtaposition of secular skepticism and spiritual yearning produced a rich tapestry of ideas, narratives, and expressions that continue to define French culture.

Individuals like Robespierre, who initially advocated for revolutionary secularism, later recognized the necessity of a spiritual component in societal cohesion. His introduction of the Cult of the Supreme Being was a testament to the enduring need for a higher moral and spiritual framework, despite the radical secularization efforts. This moral contradiction highlighted the intrinsic human inclination toward spirituality, even among the most fervent proponents of secularist ideology.

Thus, the battleground of secularism versus spirituality is etched deeply within the annals of the French Revolution. It stands as a testament to France's enduring quest to harmonize rational thought with spiritual essence. While the Revolution sought to eradicate the ancien régime's religious dominance, it inadvertently ignited a resurgence of personal spirituality, often more introspective and resilient than its institutional counterpart.

Secularism aimed to liberate the mind, yet the soul remained tethered to its eternal questions, seeking solace in mystery and transcendence. Spirituality, though battered and bent, emerged from the Revolution more introspective, personal, and diverse. France's dual identity is not a paradox but a profound narrative of coexistence, illustrating the human spirit's capacity to adapt, resist, and ultimately, harmonize conflicting ideologies.

In summation, the French Revolution, through its vigorous campaign for secularism, inadvertently paved the way for a reevaluation and revival of spirituality. It dismantled the superficial, entrenched structures of ecclesiastical power, allowing a more authentic and personal spirituality to flourish. France's dual identity, borne of this historical crucible, remains a testament to the indomitable interplay between secularism and spirituality—a dance of reason and faith that continues to shape the nation's soul.

Ongoing Tensions

France's duality has always been a compelling narrative, one that seesaws between secular ambition and inherent spirituality. The fabric of this tension was greatly embroidered by the French Revolution, which hatched a conflict between the forces of secular governance and the Catholic Church that has persisted into modernity. Like the pendulum of an ancient clock, the nation's affinity swings between Laïcité and genuine devotion, oscillating with the changing times and societal upheavals.

As we delve into the heart of these ongoing tensions, it is crucial to acknowledge the complex interplay at work. The Revolution unleashed a fervor that sought to dethrone the Church's entrenched power, replacing ecclesiastical influence with the doctrines of reason and rationality. The secular republic, born from this upheaval, took drastic steps to erode the Church's role in public life, leaving an indelible mark on the nation's collective consciousness.

Yet, beneath the fervent secularism lay an undercurrent of spiritual yearning, never fully extinguished. The very soul of France, personified by enduring landmarks like Mount Saint Michel, many a time found itself in a tug-of-war. These sacred sites stood as testament to a faith that couldn't be obliterated by mere legislative acts or fervent ideological endeavors. Herein lies the irony and the fuel for continuous strife.

In this landscape of conflict, one must not overlook the key players involved. On one side stood the proponents of a secular state, inspired by Enlightenment ideals and revolutionary zeal. On the other, the Church, which though beleaguered and stripped of much of its temporal power, still held a potent and emotional sway over the hearts of the faithful. The Revolution had weakened the Church's structural integrity, but not its core influence on those whom faith was as vital as air.

The tensions were further amplified by the stark contradictions exposed. While secular leaders proudly proclaimed the dawn of a new era devoid of religious interference, the lay faithful quietly but steadfastly upheld their spiritual traditions. This paradox birthed a peculiar duality—a France that was outwardly secular but inwardly clinging to the very essence of its Catholic roots.

Consider the ripples of legislative actions during these turbulent times. The laicization of the educational system, for instance, became an epicenter of contention. Schools, once the bastions of religious indoctrination, were gradually transformed into secular strongholds. Yet, amidst these secular institutions, remnants of religious teachings found covert ways to persist, merely changing forms rather than vanishing altogether.

Furthermore, the Concordat of 1801, a seeming reconciliation, posed no final solution but rather highlighted the precarious balance of power. It restored some recognition to the Catholic Church but under stringent controls, keeping it under the vigilant watch of the secular state. These measures neither quelled nor resolved the underlying discord but served as a salve that barely masked the deeper wounds.

This ambivalence carried forward into the future, manifesting itself in numerous sociopolitical struggles. The Church's attempts to regain lost ground, through various means ranging from grassroots movements to high-level negotiations, often clashed with rigid secular policies. Each side imbued their cause with a sense of moral righteousness, making compromise an intricate dance rather than a straightforward step.

Another facet of this tension lay in the realm of individual identity. Personal faith and public secularism created an internal schism within many French citizens. The Revolution had propagated the idea of liberty, equality, and fraternity, but for many, these ideals found no contradiction in their faith. They saw no reason why being Catholic should undermine their allegiance to the Republic or vice versa. This dual fidelity, however, often led to inner conflicts as they navigated the complex interplay between their religious and civic identities.

Moreover, the period following the Revolution saw an emboldened anti-clerical sentiment that periodically resurfaced, particularly during times of political upheaval. The Church's history, marred by instances of corruption and opulence, fed into revolutionary narratives that painted it as an anachronistic institution resistant to progress. Nonetheless, this image was constantly contested by instances of genuine piety and altruism displayed by many within the clergy and laity.

The aftermath of the Revolution also sowed seeds of skepticism towards organized religion, a sentiment that continues to linger. The public's disillusionment with ecclesiastical authorities stemmed not only from revolutionary propaganda but also real transgressions committed by those within the Church's ranks. Yet, this skepticism existed alongside a deeply rooted respect and sometimes fear for the divine, creating a labyrinthine relationship with faith.

The layers of ongoing tension between secularism and spirituality in France are countless and intricate. Each generation grapples with this duality, adding their voice to a cacophony that has persisted through centuries. Major legislative reforms, cultural shifts, and even global events have influenced this dynamic, yet the core conflict remains much the same. The Revolution irrevocably altered the terrain, but it did not erase the spiritual bedrock upon which France was partly built.

Even in contemporary times, the discourse around France's dual identity is ever pertinent. The echoes of the Revolution reverberate in modern debates over the role of religion in public life, the wearing of religious symbols, and broader issues of cultural identity. As secularism entrenches itself further, the spiritual heritage that it contests insists on making its presence felt, whether through public demonstrations of faith or subtler, more personal forms of resistance.

In summary, the ongoing tensions between France's secular state and its enduring spiritual heritage reveal a complex and multifaceted relationship. The French Revolution set the stage, but the actors—the secular government and the Catholic Church, along with the laity caught in the middle—continue to play their roles in an ever-evolving narrative. This saga is not merely a historical anecdote but a living, breathing testament to the duality that shapes France's national identity. The interplay of these forces ensures that the tapestry of French history remains rich, intricate, and perpetually unfinished.

Conclusion

The chronicles of Mount Saint Michel reverberate with a tapestry of faith and rebellion, a narrative capturing the fluid dance between secular and sacred. In scrutinizing the vestiges of the French Revolution, we uncover how this epochal upheaval etched its mark upon the spiritual heart of France. The winds of tumult and transformation that swept across the nation wrought both ruin and renewal upon the hallowed grounds of Mount Saint Michel, serving as an indelible testament to the enduring conflict between faith and freedom.

Come hither to the visage of a land scarred yet resilient, a place where pious sanctity met with earthly ambition. The French Revolution, by its very nature, struck at the root of ecclesiastical power, envisioning a realm where reason reigned supreme and religion took a subsidiary role. The de-Christianization campaigns, unfurling their fervor like a tempest, sought to sever the populace from centuries-old devotions, transforming churches into hollow shells of their former glory. Yet, amid such wreckage, hope endured, albeit in silence, nestled within the hearts of the faithful.

Mount Saint Michel found itself a fortress turned prison, an ironic twist by providence or fate, where the very guardians of faith were ensnared. The clergy, whose hands once lifted in benediction, found themselves bound by chains, their divinity questioned, their vows tested in the crucible of confinement. This paradox of punishment illuminates the Revolution's broader implications: a society grappling with its foundational mores, writhing between liberation and tradition.

Introspect upon the dual swords of Saint Michael, raised high not only in a gesture of divine defense but also in stark reminder of what the Revolution symbolized – the inexorable march towards a different kind of enlightenment, one that sought to pierce through the veil of superstition to what it deemed as unclouded truth. Thus, the martyrdom of clergy within

Mount Saint Michel etched each stone with a silent plea for patience, for perseverance through the era's spiritual impoverishment.

A silhouette of nuanced characters and shifting allegiances emerges from the annals of history. From collaborations to bitter strife, the relationship between the Church and the revolutionary government bore the marks of both pragmatism and idealism. The Concordat of 1801 speaks volumes of an uneasy reconciliation, an attempt to bridge the chasm opened by fervent secularism and lingering devotion. It informs us that despite vehement assertions to the contrary, the Revolution could not wholly disentangle the fibers of faith woven deep into the fabric of French life.

Through the retrospective lens, we see a complex panorama where the Church's influence waxed and waned. Post-revolutionary France stood at a crossroad, grappling with its own soul. Attendance in churches dwindled, authority waned, yet amidst those scorched earth terrains, seeds of renewed devotion began to sprout. The laity, rising as guardians of the sacred amidst the rubble, embarked on their quiet crusades, fostering a grassroots renaissance of religious sentiment.

Vis-à-vis the American Revolution, where the Jeffersonian model of religious liberty held sway, France's secular experiment was far more radical and contentious. The implications of this diverged approach significantly color our understanding of how far-reaching and transformative the French Revolution was for religious practice. It was not merely an abolition but a recalibration, an attempt to redefine the very essence of what it meant to be devout in a world increasingly governed by the principles of rational thought and statecraft.

A lingering gaze upon the aftermath reveals theological and philosophical ripples that extended well beyond the Revolution's temporal bounds. Catholic doctrine, hitherto seen as the immutable word, found itself under scrutiny. New winds of thought ushered in by the Revolution interrogated traditions, prompting a re-examination and, at times, a reaffirmation of faith. The revolution didn't merely sever ties; it spurred introspection and adaptation within the heart of the Church itself.

The tale of Mount Saint Michel during this period is a microcosm of the broader struggle that gripped France. It stands as a solemn witness, its stones whispering of trials and tribulations, its spires reaching towards the heavens. An emblem of resilience, this site serves not merely as a historical footnote but as an enduring beacon of faith's capacity to withstand the tempests of change.

In sum, the ecclesiastical journey through the Revolution to eventual restoration underscores a critical dialectic – the enduring and indomitable spirit of faith amidst an age of revolutionary fervor. Mount Saint Michel, with its hallowed precincts and troubled past, encapsulates this intricate dance, forever enshrining the memories of those who, in their convicts of piety and rebellion, never ceased to dream of the divine. France, this dual-natured land, continues to navigate the tensions between its secular ideals and its sacred traditions, an odyssey marked by both conflict and concord. Herein lies the essence of the Revolution's legacy on the faith of France – an ongoing testament to the country's tumultuous yet inextricable relationship with the divine.

Appendix A: Appendix

This Appendix doth serve as a repository of crucial documents and pronouncements that shaped the epoch under our scrutiny, whereby each parchment and decree doth harken back to the tides of transformation besetting the Faith of France. Herein, one shall uncover a timeline meticulously chronicling the seismic events that befell the sacred and secular realms alike during the storied French Revolution. Featured within these annals are the biographical sketches of key personages whose lives and deeds breathed fervor and consternation into the very soul of France. This compendium, with its detailed renditions, aims not solely to inform but to illuminate the repercussions that the Revolution imbued upon both the hallowed altars and the communal hearths of the French. Thus, the Appendix remains an indispensable guide, bridging the narrative threads and imbuing our exploration with a resonant depth.

Key Documents and Declarations

In the tapestry of the French Revolution, key documents and declarations emerged as monumental inscriptions, each pivotal in its own right, thus etching irrevocable marks upon the faith and soul of France. Fierce storms swept across the nation, alighting upon minds and hearts, and the written word became both sword and solace. Central to this turbulent epoch, the Civil Constitution of the Clergy of 1790 stands as a jagged precipice upon which the Church and the Revolution met in dire conflict.

Bold in intent, the Civil Constitution of the Clergy sought to restructure the Church, binding it to the state and severing the sinews of papal authority. Bishops and priests were to be elected by the populace, reducing sacred orders to mere positions of public office. Sweeping declarations mandated clerical oaths of allegiance to the nascent republic, forcing the faithful into a maelstrom of choice—allegiance to God or country. This edict not only challenged ecclesiastical order but also pierced the heart of Catholic identity, dismantling centuries-old traditions and canon law.

A profound famine of unity followed the decree, dividing clerics into "jurors" and "non-jurors," a rift that echoed throughout parishes and pews. Where there once had been a cohesive liturgical landscape, there spread a patchwork of compliance and resistance. This schism would sow not only discontent but also suspicion and persecution, as the tenets of the Revolution scrutinized orthodoxy on wiry scales and balances. Bishops, such as the venerable Monsignor de Fleury, resisted with impassioned treatises, their inked appeals becoming lanterns in a cavernous night.

Parallel to the Civil Constitution, the Declaration of the Rights of Man and of the Citizen of 1789 ignited fervor and hope, bearing the torch of Enlightenment principles. Idealistic and profound, it called for liberty, equality, and fraternity, tenets which, though unarguably compelling, left lingering shadows upon the faith. The Church, erstwhile a bastion of orientation, found its moral dominion challenged by secularism's encroaching tide.

Yet, within the ten aneurysmal years encompassing the Revolution, the National Assembly also saw fit to issue the Decree on the Abolishment of Monastic Vows in 1790. This decree, a thunderbolt to the monastic communities, shattered cloistered sanctuaries and dissolved orders whose vows tethered them not to earthly regimes but to the celestial realm. Monks and nuns were cast adrift, their holy vows transmuted into chains of condemnation by the mandate of man-made decrees.

The Papal Encyclicals of the time offered counterpoints—resounding as cries of reason and spiritual guidance in an era distorted by extremes. Pope Pius VI's *Charitas*, issued in 1791, offered admonishment and solace, urging the flock to remain steadfast amidst the cacophony. His words delineated the spiritual breaches caused by civil mandates and implored the safeguarding of ecclesiastic sanctity. His appeals to the faithful, although often smuggled past revolutionary censors, provided the diligent with a touchstone of divine law amidst man's capricious reordering.

Summons to a crisis of faith and loyalty, these documents resonate not merely as legal enactments but as urns for the ashes of a world transfixed in alchemical change. Each page unravels a context where ecclesiastical hierarchy and revolutionary zeal clash, producing a fertile ground for historical interpretation and religious introspection. The Constitution of the Year III in 1795 continued this turbulent dialogue, asserting a separation of Church and State, which although designed to temper extremes, left a dual legacy of freedom and fragmentation.

The Concordat of 1801, signed between Napoleon Bonaparte and Pope Pius VII, sought to weave together the frayed silks of ecclesiastical authority and political pragmatism. It restored some semblance of balance, acknowledging the need for a harmonious coexistence, yet it did so with stipulations and compromises that redefined the Church's role within the new order of France. Napoleon's iron quill inked a truce that, while stabilizing, re-sculpted the visage of the Church's temporal realm.

These opulent declarations and decrees were not mere parchments but living organisms, vessels of transformation that either uplifted or dismantled the faithful's worldviews. They bore significance far beyond their immediate enactment, as documents that shaped the very soul of a nation. The legacy of these written proclamations is a testament to the indelible nature of faith and governance, and the eternal interplay between the sacred and the secular. They remain testament to epochs of trial and revelation, their echoes still heard in the annals of the Church and the nation alike.

Transcending the era they were born into, these documents carried within them seeds of hope, struggle, and redemption, their impacts rippling through the unfolding centuries. Indeed, these manifestations of human resolve and divine inspiration reflect a time when the quivers of fate and faith intersected, weaving a dialogue between heaven and earthly dominions that persists even to this day. As such, they are hallowed artifacts, embodying the core struggles and triumphs of a nation's spiritual journey.

Timeline of Major Events

In the annals of the French Revolution, the confluence of divine faith and revolutionary fervor birthed a narrative profound and complex. Within this crucible, a sequence of defining moments forged the identity of France and etched their mark upon the collective consciousness of its people and its Church. As we traverse the chronological tapestry of these transformative years, we encounter a vivid tableau of human endeavor, celestial conviction, and earthly tribulation.

The year 1789 dawned with portentous clouds hovering over the French landscape. In May of that year, the Estates-General convened, an assembly summoned for the first time in over a century. This foundational gathering sought to address the dire economic crisis, but soon metamorphosed into a cauldron of revolutionary ideas. By June, the Third Estate, representing the commoners, boldly proclaimed itself the National Assembly, setting the stage for seismic societal shifts. The storming of the Bastille on July 14th also heralded an epochal upheaval. This defiant act, emblematic of the populace's wrath and burgeoning aspirations, symbolized the burgeoning rejection of autocratic dominance and clerical privilege.

August 1789 saw the promulgation of the Declaration of the Rights of Man and of the Citizen, a beacon of enlightenment ideals that championed liberty, equality, and fraternity. This document swiftly became a fulcrum around which the revolution's ethos pivoted, challenging centuries-old traditions and hierarchical structures. Amid this burgeoning fervor, the Church found itself both a spectator and an unwitting participant, as the revolution's zealous march irreversibly altered its temporal dominion.

In 1790, the Civil Constitution of the Clergy struck like a thunderbolt. This remarkable legal measure sought to subordinate the ecclesiastical establishment to the state, mandating that clergy swear an oath of allegiance to the nascent regime. Such a decree rent the very fabric of the Church, dividing the faithful into those who acquiesced and those who stood steadfast in their resignation. The corollary was the emergence of 'constitutional' and 'refractory' clergy, each embodying opposing allegiances in this moral quagmire.

As the revolution's feverish zeal reached its zenith, 1793 emerged as a year drenched in the blood of both nobility and sanctity. September marked the advent of the Reign of Terror, a period characterized by extreme measures and an insatiate guillotine. Revolutionary tribunals meted out radical justice, and no domain of society was left unscathed, including the ecclesiastical. Temples were desacralized, sacred relics profaned, and clerics martyred. The Church's expropriated properties were auctioned in feverish greed, while the orthodoxy of faith itself faced merciless persecution.

Intersecting this grim tableau, the year 1794 saw a significant, albeit fleeting, moderation in the revolutionary ardor with the fall of Maximilien Robespierre, the architect of the Reign of Terror. The ensuing Thermidorian Reaction and the subsequent Directory era ushered in a relative stabilization, allowing for a tenuous respite from the preceding maelstrom. The Church, however, remained an indelible witness to the profound scars etched into the very soul of France.

In the dawn of the new century, 1801 witnessed the consummation of the Concordat between Napoleon Bonaparte and Pope Pius VII. This accord, paradoxical in its nature, sought to mend the fractured relationship between the Church and the state. While restoring a semblance of ecclesiastical authority, it unequivocally cemented the subordination of the Church to the political prerogatives of the Napoleonic regime. This intricate interplay of power and doctrine exemplified the convolutions through which the faith navigated these treacherous waters.

Far-reaching repercussions continued to resonate throughout subsequent decades. The restoration of the Bourbon monarchy in 1814 heralded another epoch of transformation. The Catholic Church, vested anew with a degree of temporal influence, encountered an altered populace, now imbued with revolutionary ideologies and secular predilections. It was an era of contentious reconciliation, oscillating between fervent piety and profound skepticism. Thus, the delicate balance between secular aspirations and spiritual fidelity became an emblematic struggle of the restored order.

The ensuing July Monarchy and the Second Republic oscillated between convergence and divergence of ecclesiastical and civic ambitions. The Revolution of 1848, with its sweeping proclamations of universal suffrage and social reforms, further emboldened secular doctrines that sought to redefine the nexus between the temporal and the spiritual. The Second Empire, under Napoleon III, encapsulated these dynamics, as ecclesiastical institutions grappled with the compounded legacy of revolutionary secularization.

The eventual fall of the Second Empire in 1870, and the establishment of the Third Republic, crystallized into a definitive pivot towards a secular state. The Church faced an increasingly assertive laïcité, literally and metaphorically demarcating the sacred from the secular realm. The promulgation of the 1905 Law on the Separation of the Churches and State epitomized the culmination of this trajectory, legislatively enshrining the principle of secularism and redefining the French nation's identity.

As the 20th century progressed, the vestiges of revolutionary tumult receding into historical memory, the Catholic Church in France embarked on a journey of introspection and adaptation. The reverberations of the Second Vatican Council in the 1960s ushered in an era of aggiornamento, a renewal that sought to recalibrate the Church's engagement with the modern world. Yet, the undercurrent of the revolutionary legacy, with its concomitant secularism, continued to shape the contours of French religious life.

In the ebb and flow of these momentous epochs, Mount Saint Michel stood as a silent sentinel, bearing witness to the divine and the temporal interwoven within the saga of France. This bastion of faith, once a sanctuary and later a prison, encapsulated the enduring dichotomy of sublime devotion and profound despair. Through the vicissitudes of revolution and restoration, it remained a poignant symbol of the immutable spirit of faith amidst the inexorable tide of change.

The milestones of the French Revolution map a transformative journey, challenging the staunch orthodoxy of the past and ushering in a new vista of ecclesiastical and societal dynamics. As we reflect upon these edifying events, the interplay of faith and revolution, sanctity, and secularism, continues to illuminate the nuanced tapestry of human history. Each epoch, each decree, each act of defiance or fidelity, contributes to the ever-evolving narrative of the faith of France, resonating through the corridors of time.

Biographical Sketches of Key Figures

The chronicle of the French Revolution, especially in its encounters with the Church, is incomplete without an exploration of the lives involved. Herewith, we embark upon a tableau of luminous personas whose actions and virtues shaped the tumultuous era. These biographical sketches endeavor to reveal the vitality within their essence, intertwined with the fate of Mount Saint Michel and the Gallican Faith.

First, we bow to **Abbé Henri Grégoire**, a priest whose moral compass navigated through the gales of revolution. A son of humble lineage, he ascended from pastoral obscurity to become a staunch advocate for abolitionism and ecclesiastical reforms. His speeches reverberated within the National Assembly, igniting a fervor for unity and equality. With quill and voice, Grégoire championed the Civil Constitution of the Clergy, albeit with pastoral grievances. Equally revered and reviled, his presence was a beacon of resilient faith amidst nascent republicanism.

Another distinctive figure is **Georges Couthon**, a steadfast Jacobin, marked by his dedication to the revolutionary ethos. Though bound to a wheelchair by debilitating illness, Couthon's influence was unfettered. A lawyer turned revolutionary, he epitomized the antagonism towards ecclesiastical dominance, championing the Festival of the Supreme Being. His era of radicalism bore the hallmark of anti-clericalism, yet remnants of his early piety lingered. A paradoxical soul, his iconoclastic zeal could not wholly efface the indelible mark of his religious upbringing.

Also, we encounter **Madame Roland**, née Marie-Jeanne Phlipon, whose intellect and eloquence left indelible impressions upon the Girondins. Her salons were sanctuaries of Enlightenment thought, and her memoirs, a testament to her unwavering spirit. Roland's reflections on the Revolution were invariably tinted with her Catholic upbringing, as she idealized a republic founded upon moral virtue. The guillotine claimed her life, yet her legacy persisted, a confluence of piety and political fervor.

Jean-Paul Marat, the "Ami du Peuple," strides forth in stark contrast. Though predominantly known for his radicalism, Marat's early education was religious, tutored by Jesuits in his native Switzerland. An insatiable critic of the Church's opulence and inertia, Marat's newspapers fanned the flames of revolution. His words, wielded like daggers, pierced through the hypocrisy he perceived in ecclesiastical circles. His assassination rendered him a martyr of radical philosophy, his life and death marred by ecclesiastical contention.

In the annals of defiance stands **King Louis XVI**, whose reign saw both the Church's exaltation and its calamity. A monarch torn between tradition and reform, Louis grappled with his duty to uphold the ancient regime and the revolutionary tide. His pious disposition rendered the Civil Constitution of the Clergy a bitter pill. Despite his eventual deposition, his faith never wavered. The scaffold which truncated his life could not eclipse his devout legacy, as his letters from captivity revealed a heart encircled by divine hope.

Amidst this tapestry, shine the cleric **Archbishop Jean-Baptiste Gobel**, a pontiff whose pragmatic bent led him to embrace the Revolution, even at the cost of his mitre. As Archbishop of Paris, Gobel's decision to take the oath of the Civil Constitution elicited vitriol and admiration alike. His revolutionary ardor saw him donning the Phrygian cap in the National Convention, a symbol of his alignment with secular ideals. His eventual fall from grace and execution underscored the perilous straddling of ecclesiastical and revolutionary allegiances.

In counterpoint stands **Pope Pius VI**, whose papacy was besieged by the reverberations of the Revolution. An indefatigable defender of the faith, his encyclicals denounced the secularization efforts and the Civil Constitution. His correspondence with Louis XVI illuminates his entreaties for divine intervention amidst human upheaval. Pius VI bore witness to the plundering of Church properties and the French armies' desecrations. His pontificate's end epitomized the embattled Church, captured and dying in Valence, a testament to his indomitable spirit.

The courageous **Bishop Monsignor François de la Rochefoucauld** of Beauvais, vocal in the Assembly of Notables, agitated for Church reform while remaining a steadfast caretaker of his flock. His vehement opposition to ecclesiastical property confiscation rendered him a pariah to revolutionaries, yet his steadfastness was rooted in unyielding faith. Fleeing to England, he orchestrated clandestine efforts to sustain clerical morale back home. His episcopal role transcended borders, binding the spiritual hearts of expatriated Catholics.

An exalted figure of humility and erudition, **Father Jacques Cazotte** nurtured the Christian mysticism that inspired many amidst the storm. His novel "The Devil in Love" delved into metaphysical realms, intertwining faith and the supernatural. Arrested during the Terror, Cazotte faced his execution with serene detachment, his final utterance being a prayer, a witness to his unwavering faith. He epitomized the spiritual resilience that buoyed the faithful amidst the Revolutionary tempest.

Finally, we hark to the quintessential figure of **Monsieur l'Abbaye Émery**, the Superior General of the Sulpicians, who directed his congregation through the maelstrom with sagacious piety. His writings, "Letters on the Gallican Church," stand as luminous guides of ecclesiastical fidelity, confronting revolutionary ideals without surrendering spiritual integrity. Émery's clandestine seminaries preserved the priesthood's continuity, providing sanctuaries where the sacred flame of faith persisted, unextinguished by secular furies.

In summing such an eminent gallery of personages, it is evident their lives interlaced faith with fervor, shaping the Revolution's legacy. Each figure, through deeds and sacrifices, intertwines with the narrative of Mount Saint Michel's sacred precincts, embodying the eternal struggle between the temporal and the divine.